De cabo a rabo

*The Most Comprehensive Guide to Learning
Spanish Ever Written*

Vocabulario

+ Audio

David Faulkner

Now available for FREE at DavidFaulknerBooks.com:
De cabo a rabo: Vocabulario
Audiobook

Flashforward
Publishing

De cabo a rabo: Vocabulario

The Most Comprehensive Guide to Learning Spanish Ever Written

Published by Flashforward Publishing

Boulder, CO

Copyright © 2017 David Faulkner. All rights reserved.

No part of this book may be reproduced in any form or by any mechanical means, including information storage and retrieval systems without permission in writing from the publisher/author, except by a reviewer who may quote passages in a review.

All images, logos, quotes, and trademarks included in this book are subject to use according to trademark and copyright laws of the United States of America.

Library of Congress Control Number: 2017938060

ISBN: 978-0-9964497-5-5 (softcover)
ISBN: 978-0-9964497-7-9 (hardcover)

FOREIGN LANGUAGE STUDY / Spanish

QUANTITY PURCHASES: Schools, companies, professional groups, clubs, and other organizations may qualify for special terms when ordering quantities of this title. For information, please contact the author through DavidFaulknerBooks.com.

All rights reserved by David Faulkner and Flashforward Publishing

Flashforward
Publishing

Querid@ estudiante,

I designed this vocabulary guide to go hand in hand and unit by unit with *Gramática* and *Actividades*, but, of course, you can use it independently to grow your vocabulary. Although my grammar guide is intended to be everything you could ever want to know about Spanish grammar, I have no such illusions about this vocabulary guide; that's what unabridged dictionaries are for. No, this vocabulary guide is to serve as a basic to advanced resource to help you acquire enough vocabulary to have meaningful and profound conversations with native Spanish speakers from around the world on just about every topic you might come across. It, along with *Actividades*, also serves to provide context when learning the grammar. As you go out into the world to put your Spanish into practice, you will, no doubt, pick up new vocabulary that is not contained in this vocabulary guide, including synonyms for words that *are* contained here, and I hope you'll be receptive to them all.

The early units are very short, just to help you get started communicating right away. The units get progressively larger as you go and some of those earlier, smaller units are revisited to help you develop the most important topics more fully, using not only a wider range of vocabulary but also more advanced grammar. Towards the end, the units get quite large, the largest of which is the unit on medicine and the human body. When it comes to interactions between native English speakers trying to perform their jobs in Spanish with native Spanish speaking clientele, there is no profession where more is at stake than in the medical field. For my current and future students who work in medicine, I hope it gives you a good start. Regardless of your profession or motivation to learn Spanish, I'm confident this vocabulary guide will serve you well for a very long time.

Cordialmente,

David

+ Audio

P.S. Don't miss ***De cabo a rabo: Vocabulario – Audiobook***, and bonus resources like crossword puzzles and vocabulary quizzes FREE at DavidFaulknerBooks.com. For additional support, visit SpanishForTheLoveOfIt.com.

Índice

Unidad 1 – ¡Mucho gusto!

greetings and good-byes

Hola – Hello

Adiós – Bye

Hasta luego – See you later (until later)

Buenos días – Good morning

Buenas tardes – Good afternoon

Buenas noches – Good night / Good evening

to ask how someone is/feels

¿Cómo estás (tú)? – How are you? (familiar)

¿Cómo está (usted)? – How are you? (formal)

¿Qué tal? – How are things?

to answer how you are/feel

(muy) bien – (very) well

(muy) mal – (very) bad

regular – okay / fine

más o menos – okay / fine (more or less)

to show good manners

(muchas) gracias – thank you (very much)

de nada – You're welcome.

por favor – please

(Usted es) muy amable – You are very kind.

perdone / disculpe – excuse me

con permiso – excuse me (to pass by someone)

to ask someone's name and tell your name

¿Cómo te llamas (tú)? – What is your name?

(Yo) me llamo _____. – My name is _____.

¿Cómo se llama usted? – What is your name?

el nombre – name

to reciprocate a question

¿Y tú? – And you? (familiar)

¿Y usted? – And you? (formal)

introductions

Te presento a ____. – Let me introduce you to ____.

¡Mucho gusto! – It's a pleasure!

¡El gusto es mío! – The pleasure is mine!

Preséntate. – Introduce yourself.

¡Encantado! / ¡Encantada! – Delighted!

¡Igualmente! – Likewise!

titles of respect

señor (Sr.) – Mr. / sir

señora (Sra.) – Mrs. / ma'am

señorita (Srta.) – Miss.

to request and give other personal information

¿Cuál es tu número de teléfono? – What is your phone number?

Mi número (de teléfono) es _____. – My (phone) number is _____.

¿Cuándo es tu cumpleaños? – When is your birthday?

Mi cumpleaños es el _____. – My birthday is (the) _____.

¿Cuántos años tienes? – How old are you?

(Yo) tengo _____ años. – I am _____ years old.

¿De dónde eres? – Where are you from?

(Yo) soy de _____. – I am from _____.

(Hable) más despacio. – (Speak) more slowly.

(Yo) no comprendo. – I don't understand.

to say when something takes place

el / la – the
el día (*masculino*) – the day
la semana – the week
el mes – the month
el año – the year
un / una – a(n)
un día – a day
una tarde – an afternoon
hoy – today
mañana – tomorrow

próximo/a – next
el próximo lunes – next Monday
la próxima semana – next week
en – in
en dos meses – in two months
en tres días – in three days
en la mañana – in the morning
la mañana (esta mañana) – the morning (this morning)
la tarde (esta tarde) – the afternoon (this afternoon)
la noche (esta noche) – the night (tonight)

el lunes – (on) Monday
el martes – (on) Tuesday
el miércoles – (on) Wednesday
el jueves – (on) Thursday
el viernes – (on) Friday
el sábado – (on) Saturday
el domingo – (on) Sunday

enero – January
febrero – February
marzo – March
abril – April
mayo – May
junio – June

julio – July
agosto – August
septiembre – September
octubre – October
noviembre – November
diciembre – December

los números y las fechas – numbers and dates

el + *number* + de + *month*
el diez de abril – the 10th of April

el uno de – the first of
el primero de – the first of

cero (0)	diez (10)	veinte (20)	treinta (30)
uno (1)	once (11)	veintiuno (21)	treinta y uno (31)
dos (2)	doce (12)	veintidós (22)	
tres (3)	trece (13)	veintitrés (23)	
cuatro (4)	catorce (14)	veinticuatro (24)	
cinco (5)	quince (15)	veinticinco (25)	
seis (6)	dieciséis (16)	veintiséis (26)	
siete (7)	diecisiete (17)	veintisiete (27)	
ocho (8)	dieciocho (18)	veintiocho (28)	dos mil (2000)
nueve (9)	diecinueve (19)	veintinueve (29)	dos mil dieciocho (2018)

¿Cuántos/as _____ hay? – How many _____ are there?
¿Cuántos días hay en febrero? – How many days are there in February?
   Hay _____. – There is/are _____.

¿Cuál es la fecha de hoy? – What is today's date?
¿Qué día es hoy? – What day is today?
   Hoy es _____. – Today is _____.

interrogative words

¿Qué? – What?
¿Dónde? – Where?
¿Cuál? *pl.* ¿Cuáles? – Which? / What?
¿Cuándo? – When?

¿Por qué? – Why? / For what?
¿Quién? *pl.* ¿Quiénes? – Who?
¿Cómo? – How? / What?
¿Cuánto/a? – How much?
¿Cuántos/as? – How many?

Unidad 2 – lo básico

las actividades – activities
ayudar en casa – to help around the house
cocinar – to cook
dibujar – to draw
escuchar música – to listen to music
estar con amigos – to be with friends
escribir – to write
estudiar – to study
hablar (por teléfono) – to talk (on the phone)
hacer – to do
ir a la escuela – to go to school
ir al cine – to go to the movies
leer – to read
nadar – to swim
patinar – to skate
pintar – to paint
practicar deportes – to play sports
trabajar – to work
tocar la guitarra – to play the guitar
ver la televisión (tele) – to watch T.V.

to say what you like
(A mí) me gusta _____. – I like _____.
Me gusta más _____. – I like _____ more.
Me gusta mucho _____. – I like _____ a lot.
(A mí) sí me gusta _____. – I do like _____.
A mí también (me gusta). – I like it too.

to say what you don't like
(A mí) no me gusta _____. – I don't like _____.
No me gusta mucho _____. – … very much.
No me gusta nada _____. – … at all.
_____ tampoco – _____ either / neither
A mí tampoco (me gusta). – I don't (like it)
                                either.

to ask what someone likes to do
¿Qué te gusta hacer? – What do you like to do?
¿Y a ti? – And you?

to ask what someone is like
¿Eres _____? – Are you _____?
¿Cómo eres? – What are you like?
¿Cómo es ella? – What is she like?

to say what you or someone else is like
(Yo) soy _____. – I am _____.
(Ella) es _____. – She is _____.

las características – personality traits
amable – kind
artístico/a – artistic
atrevido/a – daring
callado/a – quiet
deportista – jock / plays sports
desordenado/a – disorganized / messy
divertido/a – fun
generoso/a – generous
gracioso/a – funny
honesto/a – honest
impaciente – impatient
ordenado/a – organized / neat
paciente – patient
perezoso/a – lazy
prudente – cautious
serio/a – serious
sincero/a – sincere
sociable – sociable
tacaño/a – cheap / stingy with money
trabajador/a – hard working

to verify a statement
¿De veras? – Really?
¿En serio? – Seriously?

other useful words and expressions
el (*masculino*), la (*femenino*) – the (*singular*)
los (*masculino*), las (*femenino*) – the (*plural*)
sí – yes
no – no / not
quizá – maybe
y – and
o – or
o _____ o _____ – either _____ or _____
ni _____ ni _____ – neither _____ nor _____
a veces – sometimes
muy – very
pero – but
por eso – that's why / for that
pues – well / then
también – also
tampoco – neither / either
la pregunta – question
Tengo una pregunta. – I have a question.
¿Qué significa _____? – What does _____ mean?
¿Cómo se dice _____ en español/inglés?
   – How do you say _____ in Spanish/English?

Unidad 3 – la escuela y el trabajo

la escuela – school
el almuerzo – lunch
el arte – art
las ciencias – science
las ciencias sociales – social sciences
la clase de _____ – _____ class
la educación física – P.E.
el español – Spanish
el inglés – English
las matemáticas – math
la música – music
difícil – difficult
fácil – easy
enseñar: enseña – to teach: teaches
la tarea – homework / task

la hora – hour / time of day
¿Qué hora es? – What time is it?
es / son – it is
de la mañana – in the morning
de la tarde – in the afternoon
de la noche – at night

treinta y dos (32)
treinta y tres (33)
treinta y cuatro (34)
treinta y cinco … treinta y nueve (35 – 39)

school/office supplies
la agenda – daily planner
el archivador – filing cabinet
la calculadora – calculator
el calendario – calendar
la carpeta – file folder
la computadora (compu) – computer
el cuaderno – notebook
el diccionario – dictionary
el escritorio – desk
el horario – schedule
el lápiz, *pl.* los lápices – pencil(s)
el libro – book
el marcador – marker
la mochila – backpack
el papel – paper
la pluma / el bolígrafo – pen
la regla – ruler / rule
el reloj – clock
la silla – chair

to ask and tell when something takes place
la hora – hour / time of day
empezar: empieza – to start: it starts
terminar: termina – to end: it ends
¿A qué hora? – At what time?
¿A qué hora empieza? – What times does it start?
¿A qué hora termina? – What time does it end?
    (Termina) a la una – (It ends) at one o'clock
a las dos, tres … doce – at 2:00, 3:00 … 12:00
a mediodía – at noon / midday (not exact time)
a medianoche – at midnight / in the middle of the night
el semestre – semester
el primer semestre – first semester
el segundo semestre – second semester
la primera semana – the first week

Es la una (y veinte). – It is 1:00 o'clock (1:20).
Son las dos, tres, doce (y cuarenta). – It is _____ (:40).
(y) cuarto – quarter (15 minutes)
(y) media – half (30 minutes)
Son las once y media de la noche. – It's 11:30 PM.

cuarenta (40)
cuarenta y uno … cuarenta y nueve (41 – 49)
cincuenta (50)
cincuenta y uno … cincuenta y nueve (51 – 59)

el horario – schedule
la cita – appointment
la escuela – school
la reunión – meeting
el trabajo – work / job
importante – important

people at school or at work
el colega / la colega – colleague
el consejero / la consejera – counselor
el compañero / la compañera – companion / mate
el director / la directora – principal / director
el empleado / la empleada – employee
el estudiante / la estudiante – student
el jefe / la jefa – (the) boss
el maestro / la maestra – (the) teacher
el mentor / la mentora – mentor
el tutor / la tutora – tutor
con – with
Mucho gusto en conocerte. – It's a pleasure to meet you.

la posesión – possession

tener: (yo) tengo – to have: I have
    (tú) tienes   you have
mi(s) – my   nuestro/a(s) – our
tu(s) – your   vuestro/a(s) – your
su(s) – his / her   su(s) – their
    – your (Ud.)   – your (Uds.)

mi jefe – my boss   mis maestros – my teachers
tu jefe – your boss   tus colegas – your colleagues
nuestro jefe – our (male) boss
nuestra jefa – our (female) boss
su jefa – his/her/their (female) boss

Tengo mis cuadernos en mi mochila. – I have my notebooks in my backpack.

to ask and say people's names

¿Cómo te llamas? – What is your name? (What do you call yourself?)
    Yo me llamo _____. – My name is _____. (I call myself _____.)
¿Cuál es tu nombre? – What is your name?
    Mi nombre es _____. – My name is _____.
¿Cómo se llama él/ella? – What is his/her name? (What does he/she call himself/herself?)
    Él/ella se llama _____. – His/her name is _____. (He/she calls himself/herself _____.)
¿Cuál es su nombre? – What is his/her name?
    Su nombre es _____. – His/her name is _____.
¿Cómo se llama tu jefa? – What is your boss's name?
¿Cuál es el nombre de tu jefa? – What is your boss's name?
presentar – to present / to introduce (a person)   "Te presento a mi amigo."
el apodo / el sobrenombre / el mote – nickname

to say what something is for (its purpose)

para – for
Tengo un lápiz para la clase. – I have a pencil for the class.
¿Tienes tu computadora para la reunión? – Do you have your computer for the meeting?

to ask and say what people need

necesitar: (yo) necesito – to need: I need
        (tú) necesitas   you need

Necesito un cuaderno para la reunión. – I need a notebook for the meeting.
¿Necesitas una agenda para el trabajo? – Do you need a daily planner for work (for the job)?

quantity

mucho/a – a lot of / much
muchos/as – a lot of / many
poco/a – a little
pocos/as – a few
un/una – a(n)

¿Tienes mucha tarea? – Do you have a lot of homework?
¿Tienes muchas plumas? – Do you have a lot of pens?
Tengo poca tarea. – I have a little homework.
Tengo una pluma. – I have a pen. / I have one pen.

other useful words and expressions

favorito/a – favorite
más – more / most / else (¿Qué más? – What else?)
menos – less / fewer / least
de – of / from
de la escuela – from the school
a – to (direction)
a la escuela – to the school
de lunes a viernes – from Monday to Friday
                  – Monday through Friday

to show regret or empathy

Lo siento (mucho). – I'm (so) sorry.

location

aquí – here
    Aquí está. – Here it is.
allí – there
    Allí está. – There it is.

Unidad 4 – los pasatiempos

to describe how someone is or feels
estar – to be (physical states and emotions)
¿Cómo estás? – How are you?
   Estoy enfermo/a. – I am sick.
      aburrido/a – bored
      cansado/a – tired / worn out
      contento/a – happy
      deprimido/a – depressed
      emocionado/a – excited
      frustrado/a – frustrated
      harto/a – fed up
      listo/a – ready
      nervioso/a – nervous
      ocupado/a – busy
      preocupado/a – worried
      triste – sad

to ask and say where someone is
estar – to be (location)
¿Dónde estás? – Where are you?
   Estoy en el parque. – I am at the park.

-ar verbs (regulars)
alquilar / rentar (videos) – to rent (videos)
bailar – to dance
caminar – to walk
cantar – to sing
cocinar – to cook
enseñar – to teach
escuchar (música) – to listen to (music)
esquiar – to ski
estudiar – to study
fumar – to smoke
hablar – to speak / to talk
limpiar (la casa) – to clean (the house)
manejar (un carro) – to drive (a car)
mirar (la tele) – to watch (T.V.) / to look at
montar (en bicicleta) – to ride (a bicycle)
nadar – to swim
pasar (tiempo) – to pass / to spend (time)
pescar – to fish
pintar – to paint
platicar / charlar – to talk / to chat
preparar (la cena) – to prepare (dinner)
tocar – to touch / to play an instrument
trabajar – to work
usar (la computadora) – to use
viajar – to travel

-er/-ir verbs (regulars)
aprender – to learn
abrir – to open
comer – to eat
correr – to run
asistir (a clase) – to attend (class)
beber (jugo) – to drink (juice)
escribir (una carta) – to write (a letter)
leer (un libro) – to read (a book)
vivir (en la ciudad) – to live (in the city)

-ar/-er/-ir verbs (irregulars)
ir – to go
   a una fiesta – to go to a party
   de compras – to go shopping
jugar (u → ue) – to play
   (al) básquetbol – to play basketball
   (al) béisbol – to play baseball
   (al) fútbol – to play soccer
   (al) fútbol americano – to play football
   (al) tenis – to play tennis
   (a los) videojuegos – to play videogames
   (al) voleibol – to play volleyball
pensar (e → ie) (que) – to think (that)
poder (o → ue) – to be able
preferir (e → ie) – to prefer
querer (e → ie) – to want
saber (yo sé) – to know (information)
tener (yo tengo) (e → ie) – to have
ver (yo veo) – to see / to watch

to ask and say where someone is going
ir: (yo) voy – to go: I'm going / I go
   (tú) vas   you're going / you go
a – to
al (a + el) / a la – to the
de – from / of
del (de + el) / de la – from the
el campo – field / countryside
el centro comercial – mall
el gimnasio – gym
el parque – park
el parque de diversiones – amusement park
la piscina / la alberca – swimming pool
la playa – beach
¿Adónde? – Where to? / To where?
¿Adónde vas? – Where are you going?
   Voy a la playa. – I am going to the beach.

to say with whom you do an activity
con – with
    conmigo – with me
    contigo – with you
    con él, ella, Ud. – with him, her, you
    con nosotros/as – with us
    con vosotros/as – with you (all) (Spain)
    con ellos/as, Uds. – with them, you (all)
sin – without
    sin mí – without me
    sin ti – without you
    sin él, ella, Ud. – without him, her, you
    sin nosotros/as – without us
    sin vosotros/as – without you (all) (Spain)
    sin ellos/as, Uds. – without them, you (all)
el amigo / la amiga – friend
la familia – family
solo/a – alone
juntos/as – together

to extend, accept, or decline invitations
tal vez – perhaps
posiblemente – possibly
probablemente – probably
poder: (yo) puedo – to be able: I can
      (tú) puedes   you can
querer: (yo) quiero – to want: I want
      (tú) quieres   you want
¡Cómo no! / ¡Por supuesto! – Of course!
¡Claro que sí! – Of course!
¡Claro que no! – Of course not!
de nada / por nada – You're welcome.

to say when you do an activity
la estación, *pl.* las estaciones – season(s)
la primavera – spring
el verano – summer
el otoño – fall / autumn
el invierno – winter
el lunes, el martes . . . – (on) Monday, Tuesday
los lunes, los martes . . . – (on) Mondays, etc.
el fin de semana – (on) the weekend
los fines de semana – (on) the weekends
después de (la escuela) – after (school)
(en / por) la mañana – (in) the morning
         la tarde – (in) the afternoon
         la noche – (at) night
generalmente – generally
hoy no – not today
mañana – tomorrow
todos los días – every day

las exclamaciones – exclamations
¡No me digas! – You don't say!
¡A poco! – No way! / Say it ain't so!
¡Genial! – Awesome! / Sweet!
¡Qué lástima! – What a pity!
¡Qué pena! – What a shame! / How sad!

other useful words and phrases
la voz, *pl.* las voces – voice(s)
algo – something
nada – nothing
    – anything (in a negative sentence)
      Ej. No tengo nada.
el pasatiempo – pastime
que – that
porque – because
¿por qué? – why?
¿por qué no? – why not?
ir + a + *infinitivo* – to be going *to* _____
para + *infinitivo* – in order *to* _____
    para nadar – in order to swim
después de + *infinitivo* – after _____*ing*
    después de nadar – after swimming
antes de + *infinitivo* – before _____*ing*
    antes de nadar – before swimming
sin + *infinitivo* – without _____*ing*
    sin nadar – without swimming

Unidad 5 – la comida

las comidas – meals

comer – to eat (lunch)

beber / tomar – to drink

desayunar – to eat breakfast

almorzar (o → ue) – to eat lunch

cenar – to eat dinner / to dine

la cena – dinner

la comida – food / lunch

la (comida) chatarra – junk (food)

el desayuno – breakfast

la merienda – afternoon snack

la botana – snack

el aperitivo – appetizer

los refrigerios – refreshments

la comida – food

el arroz – rice

el atún – tuna

el bistec – steak

la carne – meat (often beef)

el cereal – cereal

la ensalada – salad

las frutas – fruits

   el aguacate / la palta – avocado

   el arándano – blueberry / cranberry

   la ciruela – plum

   el durazno / el melocotón – peach

   la frambuesa – raspberry

   la fresa / la frutilla – strawberry

   el limón – lemon / lime

   la manzana – apple

   el melón – melon (cantaloupe, honeydew)

   la naranja – orange

   la nectarina – nectarine

   la pera – pear

   la piña – pineapple

   el plátano / la banana – banana

   la sandía – watermelon

   el tomate – tomato

   la toronja – grapefruit

   la uva – grape

   la zarzamora (mora) – blackberry

los frutos secos / las nueces – nuts

   la almendra – almond

   el anacardo – cashew

   el cacahuate / el maní – peanut

   la nuez – walnut

   el pistacho – pistachio

el guisado – stew

la hamburguesa – hamburger

la hamburguesa con queso – cheeseburger

el huevo – egg

el jamón – ham

la mayonesa – mayonnaise

la mostaza – mustard

el pan – bread

   el pan tostado – toast

la papa / la patata – potato

   las papas al horno – baked potatoes

   las papas fritas – french fries

el pescado – fish

el pollo – chicken

el puerco – pork

el queso – cheese

la sal y la pimienta – salt and pepper

el sándwich / la torta – sandwich

   de jamón – ham sandwich

   de queso – cheese sandwich

la sopa – soup

   de pollo – chicken soup

   de tomate – tomato soup

   de verduras – vegetable soup

las verduras / los vegetales – vegetables

   el ajo – garlic

   el apio – celery

   la berenjena – eggplant

   el brócoli / el brécol – broccoli

   la calabaza – pumpkin / squash

   el calabacín – zucchini

   la cebolla – onion

   los chícharos / los guisantes – peas

   el chile – chili pepper

   la col / el repollo – cabbage

   la col rizada – kale

   la coliflor – cauliflower

   los espárragos – asparagus

   las espinacas – spinach

   las habichuelas verdes – green beans

   la lechuga – lettuce

   el maíz – corn

   el pepinillo – pickle

   el pepino – cucumber

   el pimiento – bell pepper

   los repollitos de Bruselas – Brussels sprouts

   la zanahoria – carrot

el yogur – yogurt

las bebidas – drinks
el agua (*femenino*) – water
el café – coffee
el jugo de naranja – orange juice
el jugo de manzana – apple juice
la leche – milk
el licuado / el batido – smoothie
la limonada – lemonade
el refresco / la gaseosa – soft drink
el té (caliente) – (hot) tea
el té helado / el té frío – iced tea

el postre – dessert
el chocolate – chocolate
el helado – ice cream
la paleta – popsicle
el pastel – cake

las descripciones – descriptions
bueno/a (para la salud) – good (for your health)
malo/a (para la salud) – bad (for your health)
delicioso/a / sabroso/a – delicious / tasty
asqueroso/a – disgusting
auténtico/a – authentic

likes or preferences
más o menos – more or less
me encanta(n) – I love it (them)
me gusta(n) – I like it (them)
preferir (e → ie) – to prefer

la opinión – opinion
creer – to believe / to think
Creo que sí. – I believe so. / I think so.
Creo que no. – I don't think so.
¡Qué asco! – How disgusting!
¡Guácala! – Yuck!

la frecuencia – frequency
nunca – never
  – ever (in a negative sentence)
    Ej. Ella no quiere ir nunca.
siempre – always
todos los días – every day
una vez – once / one time
dos veces – twice / two times
muchas veces – a lot / many times
de vez en cuando – from time to time
normalmente – normally

¿Cuándo?
ahora – now
a tiempo – on time
durante – during
mientras – while
pronto – soon
tarde – late
temprano – early

otras palabras y expresiones útiles
algo – something
nada – nothing
  – anything (in a negative sentence)
    Ej. No quiero nada.
alguno/a(s) – some
algún – some (before *singular*, *masculine noun*)
  algún restaurante – some restaurant
ninguno/a – none (effectively no *plural* form)
  – any (in a negative sentence)
    Ej. No quiero ninguna bebida.
ningún – no (before *singular*, *masculine noun*)
  ningún restaurante – no restaurant
    – any (in a negative sentence)
    Ej. No quiero ir a ningún restaurante.
unos / unas – some
como – like / as
¿no? / ¿verdad? – right?
si – if / whether (no accent mark)
la experiencia – experience
tener hambre – to be hungry
tener sed – to be thirsty
los dos / las dos – both
mismo/a – same

Unidad 6 – la gente y las descripciones

la familia – family
los abuelos: el abuelo – grandpa
             la abuela – grandma
los hermanos: el hermano – brother
             la hermana – sister
los hijos: el hijo – son
          la hija – daughter
los nietos: el nieto – grandson
          la nieta – granddaughter
los padres: el padre (papá) – father (dad)
          la madre (mamá) – mother (mom)
los primos: el primo – cousin
          la prima – cousin
los tíos: el tío – uncle
          la tía – aunt
el hijo único / la hija única – only child
los gemelos / las gemelas – twins

las descripciones – descriptions
ser + *adjetivo* – to be _____
alto/a – tall
antipático/a – mean
bajo/a – short
bonito/a – pretty / good-looking
cariñoso/a – affectionate
delgado/a – thin
feo/a – ugly
gordo/a – fat
grande – big / large
guapo/a – good-looking (handsome, gorgeous)
inteligente – intelligent
joven, *pl.* jóvenes – young
mayor, *pl.* mayores – older / greater
menor, *pl.* menores – younger / lesser
pelirrojo/a – redhead
pequeño/a – small
simpático/a – nice
viejo/a – old
tener + *sustantivo* – to have _____
el pelo – hair

canoso – gray	corto – short
castaño – brown	largo – long
negro – black	liso – straight
rubio – blonde	rizado – curly

los ojos – eyes
    azules – blue eyes
    verdes – green eyes
    marrones – brown eyes

la gente – people
el / la adolescente – adolescent / teenager
el / la adulto/a – adult
el bebé – baby (regardless of gender or sex)
el chico / el muchacho – boy
la chica / la muchacha – girl
el hombre – man
la mujer – woman
el / la niño/a – child
la persona – person (regardless of gender or sex)

to ask and say what someone is like
¿Cómo es Laura? – What is Laura like?
    Ella es _____. – She is _____.
¿Cómo son Laura y Paco? – What are they like?
    Son _____. – They are _____.

to make comparisons
más + *adjetivo* + que – more _____ than
menos + *adjetivo* + que – less _____ than
mayor que – older than
menor que – younger than

la edad – age
¿Cuántos años tiene él? – How old is he?
    Él tiene ____ años. – He is _____ years old.

sesenta (60)	noventa (90)
setenta (70)	cien (100)
ochenta (80)	ciento uno (101)

las mascotas – pets
el gato – cat
el perro – dog

la posesión – possession
de – of
de mi hermano – my brother's (of my brother's)
el gato de mi tío – my uncle's cat
tener (yo tengo) (e → ie) – to have

el número – number
¿Cuántos/as? – How many?
alguien – someone
nadie – no one
    – anyone (in a negative sentence)
    Ej. No hay nadie aquí.
sólo / solo / solamente – only
todos/as – every / all / everyone

Unidad 7 – la ropa

articles of clothing
la blusa – blouse
la bolsa – bag / purse
el calcetín, *pl.* los calcetines – sock(s)
la camisa – shirt
la camiseta – T-shirt
la chaqueta / la chamarra – jacket
la corbata – tie / necktie
la falda – skirt
los jeans – jeans (pronounced as in English)
los pantalones (cortos) – pants (shorts)
la ropa – clothing / clothes
la sudadera – sweatshirt
el suéter – sweater
el traje – suit
los (zapatos de) tenis – tennis shoes
el vestido – dress
los zapatos – shoes

las descripciones – descriptions
el color – color
¿De qué color es _____? – What color is _____?
amarillo/a – yellow
anaranjado/a – orange
azul, *pl.* azules – blue
blanco/a – white
gris, *pl.* grises – gray
marrón, *pl.* marrones – brown
morado/a – purple
negro/a – black
rojo/a – red
rosado/a – pink
verde – green
nuevo/a – new
¡Qué + *adjetivo*! – How _____!

specific items
ese (*masc.*) / esa (*fem.*) / eso (*neutro*) – that
esos / esas – those
este (*masc.*) / esta (*fem.*) / esto (*neutro*) – this
estos / estas – these
otro/a – other / another

places to shop for clothing
el almacén – warehouse
la tienda de descuentos – discount store
la tienda de ropa – clothing store
la zapatería – shoe store

de compras – out shopping
buscar – to look for
comprar – to buy
contar (o → ue) – to count
costar (o → ue) – to cost
desear – to want / to desire
encontrar (o → ue) – to find
llevar – to wear
pagar – to pay
venir (yo vengo) (e → ie) – to come
para – for (intended recipient)
    para mí – for me
    para ti – for you
    para él, ella, Ud. – for him, her, you
por – for (in exchange for)
    por $15 – for $15
el precio – price
el dinero – money
ciento un(o)/una, etc. – one hundred one, etc.
¿Cuánto cuesta _____? – How much does ____ cost?
    Cuesta _____. – It costs _____.
¿Cuánto cuestan ____? How much do ____ cost?
    Cuestan _____. – They cost _____.
el dólar, *pl.* los dólares – dollar(s)
4 dólares <u>con</u> 5 centavos – 4 dollars <u>and</u> 5 cents
la ganga – bargain
¡Qué ganga! – What a bargain!
barato/a – cheap / inexpensive
caro/a – expensive
gratis / gratuito/a – free (no cost)

la gente – people
el dependiente / la dependienta – store clerk
el / la joven, *pl.* los / las jóvenes – youngster(s)

location
por aquí – this way / around here
por allí – that way / around there
por todas partes – everywhere
por ninguna parte – nowhere / anywhere (negative)

to make comparisons
más + *adjetivo* + que – more _____ than
menos + *adjetivo* + que – less _____ than
mejor que – better than
peor que – worse than
tan + *adjetivo* + como – as _____ as
tanto/a + *sustantivo* + como – as much _____ as

los números cardinales – cardinal numbers

(1) uno	(30) treinta	(200) doscientos
(2) dos	(31) treinta y uno	(268) doscientos sesenta y ocho
(3) tres	(32) treinta y dos	(300) trescientos
(4) cuatro	(33) treinta y tres	(383) trescientos ochenta y tres
(5) cinco	(34) treinta y cuatro	(400) cuatrocientos
(6) seis	(35) treinta y cinco	(405) cuatrocientos cinco
(7) siete	(40) cuarenta	(500) quinientos
(8) ocho	(41) cuarenta y uno	(520) quinientos veinte
(9) nueve	(42) cuarenta y dos	(600) seiscientos
(10) diez	(43) cuarenta y tres	(699) seiscientos noventa y nueve
(11) once	(44) cuarenta y cuatro	(700) setecientos
(12) doce	(45) cuarenta y cinco	(777) setecientos setenta y siete
(13) trece	(50) cincuenta	(800) ochocientos
(14) catorce	(51) cincuenta y uno	(801) ochocientos uno
(15) quince	(52) cincuenta y dos	(900) novecientos
(16) dieciséis	(53) cincuenta y tres	(914) novecientos catorce
(17) diecisiete	(54) cincuenta y cuatro	(1,000) mil
(18) dieciocho	(60) sesenta	(1,928) mil novecientos veintiocho
(19) diecinueve	(66) sesenta y seis	(2,000) dos mil
(20) veinte	(70) setenta	(2,004) dos mil cuatro
(21) veintiuno	(77) setenta y siete	(3,000) tres mil
(22) veintidós	(80) ochenta	(4,000) cuatro mil
(23) veintitrés	(88) ochenta y ocho	(10,000) diez mil
(24) veinticuatro	(90) noventa	(25,000) veinticinco mil
(25) veinticinco	(99) noventa y nueve	(50,000) cincuenta mil
(26) veintiséis	(100) cien	(100,000) cien mil
(27) veintisiete	(101) ciento uno	(1,000,000) un millón
(28) veintiocho	(110) ciento diez	(1,000,000,000) mil millones
(29) veintinueve	(132) ciento treinta y dos	(1,502,000,000) mil quinientos dos millones

¡Ojo! <u>un</u> vestid<u>o</u> (1), veinti<u>ún</u> vestid<u>os</u> (21), treinta y <u>un</u> añ<u>os</u> (31), ciento <u>un</u> dólar<u>es</u> (101)
un<u>a</u> camis<u>a</u> (1), veintiun<u>a</u> camis<u>as</u> (21), treinta y un<u>a</u> seman<u>as</u> (31), doscient<u>as</u> un<u>a</u> cos<u>as</u> (201)

(1/2) la mitad	(1/3) un tercio	(1/4) un cuarto	(1/5) una quinta parte
una mitad	(2/3) dos tercios	(3/4) tres cuartos	(2/5) dos quintas partes

direct-object pronouns

lo – it (*masculino*)   los – them (*masculino*) (*masculino* and *femenino*)
la – it (*femenino*)   las – them (*femenino*)

otras palabras y expresiones útiles

la fiesta – party
¿Qué tal? – How are things?
¿Qué tal _____? – How about _____?
¿Cómo te queda? – How does it fit you?
 Me queda bien. – It fits me well.
¿Qué te parece? – What do you think (of it)?
 Me parece bien. – It seems good to me.
¡Feliz cumpleaños! – Happy birthday!

igual / lo mismo – the same
(me) da igual – it's all the same (to me)
¡Vaya! / ¡Anda! – Wow!
A ver … – Let's see …
cuando – when
hasta – until
para + *infinitivo* – in order to _____
perdone (Ud.) / disculpe (Ud.) – excuse me

Unidad 8 – las vacaciones

las vacaciones – vacation
estar de vacaciones – to be on vacation
ir de vacaciones – to go on vacation

places to visit on vacation
la catarata / la cascada – waterfall
la catedral – cathedral
el centro – center
la ciudad – city
el lago – lake
los lugares de interés – places of interest
el mar – ocean / sea
la montaña – mountain
el museo – museum
el país – country
la pirámide – pyramid
el río – river
la selva tropical – rain forest
las ruinas (el sitio arqueológico) – ruins

las actividades – activities
andar / pasear – to go (around, about) / to walk
bajar – to go down / to lower
bucear – to SCUBA dive
descansar – to rest
esquiar (i → í) – to ski
explorar – to explore
llevar – to carry / to wear
los recuerdos – souvenirs
sacar fotos – to take photos
    la fotografía (foto) – photograph (photo)
subir – to go up / to rise / to raise
tomar el sol – to sunbathe
visitar – to visit

planning a vacation
pensar (e → ie) + *infinitivo* – to plan *to* _____
regresar – to return / to go back
entrar (en) – to enter (into)
salir (de) – to leave (from)
    (yo) salgo – I leave
querer (e → ie) + *infinitivo* – to want *to* _____
poder (o → ue) + *infinitivo* – to be able *to* _____
ir + a + *infinitivo* – to be going *to* _____
necesitar – to need
traer – to bring
    (yo) traigo – I bring
repetir (e → i) – to repeat

things to take on vacation
el abrigo – coat
las gafas de sol – sunglasses
las botas – boots
el bronceador – suntan lotion
la bufanda – scarf
la cámara – camera
la gorra – baseball cap
los guantes – gloves
el impermeable – rain jacket
la maleta – suitcase
el (los) paraguas – umbrella(s) (for rain)
el parasol – umbrella to block the sun
el pasaporte – passport
la toalla – towel
el traje de baño – bathing suit

el tiempo – weather
¿Qué tiempo hace? – What's the weather like?
Hace buen tiempo. – It's good weather.
Hace calor. – It's hot.
Hace fresco. – It's cool. / It's chilly.
Hace frío. – It's cold.
Hace mal tiempo. – It's bad weather.
Hace sol. – It's sunny.
Hace viento. – It's windy.
Hace 32 grados. – It's 32 degrees.
Está nublado. – It's cloudy.
Llueve. – It's raining. / It rains.
Está lloviendo. – It's raining.
Nieva. – It's snowing. / It snows.
Está nevando. – It's snowing.
la lluvia – rain
la nieve – snow
la nube – cloud
el sol – sun
el viento – wind

¿Adónde vas?
a ninguna parte – nowhere / anywhere (negative)
a todas partes – everywhere
aquí (precise) / acá (vague) – here
allí / ahí (precise) / allá (vague) – there

ongoing action
estar + *gerundio* (-*ing* form) – to be _____*ing*
¿Qué estás haciendo? – What are you doing?
    Estoy descansando. – I am resting.

Unidad 9 – la casa y los quehaceres

to say where someone lives
cerca (de) – near / close (to)
lejos (de) – far (from)
al lado (de) – next to / to the side (of)
vivir – to live
en – in / on / at

houses or apartments
el alquiler / la renta – rent
el apartamento – apartment
el baño – bathroom
la casa (de _3_ pisos) – (_3_ story) house
el césped / el sacate (zacate) – lawn
la cocina – kitchen
el comedor – dining room
el cuarto – room
el dormitorio / la habitación / la recámara
    – bedroom
el elevador / el ascensor – elevator
las escaleras – stairs / staircase
el garaje / la cochera – garage
el jardín (delantero, trasero) – (front, back) yard
el lavadero – laundry room
la pared – wall
el pasillo – hallway (hall)
el patio – patio
el (primer, segundo) piso – (first, second) floor
el porche – porch
la sala – living room
la sala de estar – family room
el sótano – basement

household items
la alfombra – carpet
la bañera / la tina – bathtub
la cama – bed
la chimenea – chimney / fireplace
el coche / el carro – car
la cómoda – dresser
    el cajón, *pl.* los cajones – drawer(s)
el (los) cortacésped – lawnmower(s)
la cortina – curtain
las cosas – things / stuff
el cuadro – picture (usually framed)
la ducha – shower
los electrodomésticos – appliances
la escoba – broom
el escritorio – desk

el espejo – mirror
el estante – shelf / bookshelf
el estéreo – stereo
    la bocina / el parlante – speaker
la estufa – stove
el fregadero – kitchen sink
el guardarropa / el clóset – closet
el horno – oven
el (horno de) microondas – microwave (oven)
el inodoro / el retrete / la taza – toilet
la lámpara – lamp
el lavabo / el (los) lavamanos – bathroom sink(s)
la lavadora – washing machine
el (los) lavaplatos – dishwasher(s)
la mesa – table
los muebles – furniture
el piso / el suelo – floor
el póster, *pl.* los pósters / el cartel – poster(s)
la puerta – door
el reproductor de CD/DVD – CD/DVD player
el refrigerador (refri) – refrigerator (fridge)
la secadora – clothes dryer
la silla – chair
el sillón, *pl.* los sillones – armchair(s)
el sofá (*masculino*) – couch / sofa
el tapete – rug
el televisor – TV set
la ventana – window

las descripciones
antiguo/a – old / antique
bastante – quite / rather (*adverb*)
cómodo/a – comfortable
cuadrado/a – square
de cuero – (made) of leather
de madera – wooden / (made) of wood
de metal – (made) of metal
de plástico – (made) of plastic
de vidrio – (made) of glass
grande – large / big
incómodo/a – uncomfortable
limpio/a – clean
moderno/a – modern
nuevo/a – new
pequeño/a – small
real – real / royal
redondo/a – round
sucio/a – dirty

los colores – colors
amarillo/a – yellow
anaranjado/a / naranja – orange
azul – blue
blanco/a – white
gris – gray
marrón, *pl.* marrones – brown
morado/a – purple
    claro – light purple
    oscuro – dark purple
negro/a – black
rojo/a – red
rosado/a / rosa – pink
verde – green
    claro – light green
    oscuro – dark green

los quehaceres (de la casa) – chores
arreglar – to fix / to straighten / to tidy
ayudar – to help
barrer – to sweep
cortar (el césped) – to cut / to mow (the lawn)
desempolvar – to dust
hacer – to do / to make
    (yo) hago – I do / I make
hacer la cama – to make the bed
lavar (la ropa, los platos)
    – to wash (clothes, dishes)
limpiar (el baño) – to clean (the bathroom)
pasar la aspiradora – to vacuum
planchar (la ropa) – to iron (clothes)
poner – to put / to place / to set
    (yo) pongo – I put / I place / I set
poner la mesa – to set the table
preparar – to prepare
    el desayuno – to prepare breakfast
    el almuerzo – to prepare lunch
    la cena – to prepare dinner
quitar la mesa – to clear the table
sacar la basura – to take out the trash
usar – to use

las preferencias – preferences
preferir (e → ie) – to prefer
querer (e → ie) – to want

la obligación – obligation
tener que + *infinitivo* – to have *to* _____
deber + *infinitivo* – to ought *to* (should) _____
necesitar + *infinitivo* – to need *to* _____

la frecuencia – frequency
¿con qué frecuencia? – how often?
a menudo / muchas veces – often
a veces – sometimes
cada – each / every
(casi) nunca – (almost) never
(casi) siempre – (almost) always
constantemente – constantly
de vez en cuando – from time to time
frecuentemente – frequently
generalmente – generally
normalmente – normally
(casi) todos los días – (almost) every day
los lunes – (on) Mondays
los fines de semana – (on) the weekends
después de + *infinitivo* – after _____*ing*
antes de + *infinitivo* – before _____*ing*

otras palabras útiles
hay – there is / there are
    un / una – a(n)
    uno / una – one
    dos – two
    tres – three
ándale (pues) – get to it (then)
ambos/as – both
el gancho – hanger / hook
el (los) pasamanos – handrail(s)

los adjetivos posesivos – possessive adjectives

mi(s) – my	nuestro(s)/a(s) – our
tu(s) – your	vuestro(s)/a(s) – your
su(s) – his / her	su(s) – their
– your (Ud.)	– your (Uds.)

los complementos directos – direct-object
                          pronouns
lo – it (*masculino*)
la – it (*femenino*)
los – them (*masculino*) (*masculino* y *femenino*)
las – them (*femenino*)

Unidad 10 – el cuerpo humano y las enfermedades

las partes del cuerpo – parts of the body
la boca – mouth
el brazo – arm
la cabeza – head
la cara – face
el cuello – neck
el cuerpo – body
el dedo – finger
los dientes – teeth
la espalda – back
el estómago – stomach
la garganta – throat
el hombro – shoulder
la lengua – tongue
la mano (*femenino*) – hand
la nariz – nose
el oído – inner ear
la oreja – outer ear
el ojo – eye
el pecho – chest
el pelo / el cabello – hair
el pie – foot
el dedo de pie – toe
la pierna – leg
la rodilla – knee
derecho/a – right
izquierdo/a – left

ways to maintain good health
descansar – to rest
dormir (o → ue) – to sleep
hacer ejercicio – to exercise
la salud – health
estar sano/a – to be healthy (people)
ser saludable – to be healthy (food)
las vitaminas – vitamins

preguntas básicas – basic questions
¿Qué te duele? – What hurts (you)?
¿Qué (síntomas) tienes?
   – What (symptoms) do you have?
¿Cómo te sientes? – How do you feel?
¿Qué te pasa? – What's happening (to you)?

las profesiones médicas – medical professions
el / la dentista – dentist
el / la doctor/a / médico/a – doctor
el / la enfermero/a – nurse
el / la farmacéutico/a – pharmacist

to talk about your medical problems
¡Ay! – Ouch! / Ow!
el dolor – pain
doler (o → ue) – to ache / to hurt
la enfermedad – sickness / illness / disease
la fiebre – fever
la gripe / la gripa – flu
la tos – cough
sentir (e → ie) – to feel (used with *nouns*)
Tengo … – I have … / Siento … – I feel …
   dolor de cabeza – a headache
   dolor de estómago – a stomachache
   dolor de garganta – a sore throat
   dolor de muelas – a toothache (molars)
   dolor de oído – an earache
   alergias – allergies
   fiebre – a fever
   gripe – the flu
   mocos – mucous
   resfrío / resfriado – a cold
   tos – a cough
Tengo … – I am …
   ___ años – ___ years old
   hambre – hungry
   sed – thirsty
   calor – hot
   frío – cold
   sueño – sleepy
sentirse (e → ie) – to feel (used with
                    adjectives and *adverbs*)
estar – to be (physical or mental state)
Estoy … – I am … / Me siento … – I feel …
   enfermo/a – sick
   bien – well
   fatal – awful
   horrible – horrible
   resfriado/a – sick (with a cold)
   mal – bad
   (aun) mejor – (even) better
   (aun) peor – (even) worse
   terrible – terrible
así – like this / like that (in this/that way)

las opiniones – opinions
creer (que) – to believe (that)
pensar (e → ie) (que) – to think (that)
que – that (no accent mark)
¿no? – right? (affirmative sentence only)
¿verdad? – right? (affirmative or negative)

to talk about duration

¿Cuánto (tiempo) hace que _____?
    – How long has it been that _____?
Hace tres días que _____.
    – It has been three days that _____.
ahora / ya – now
todavía – still / yet
ya no – not now
ya no más – not any more

what to do when you are sick

la clínica – clinic / doctor's office
la enfermería – nurse's office
el hospital – hospital
la farmacia – pharmacy
hacer una cita – to make an appointment
llamar – to call
    hacer una llamada – to make a call
    marcar – to dial (a phone number)
    oprimir – to press (a button)
    colgar (o → ue) – to hang up (the phone)
    descolgar (o → ue) – to pick up (the phone)
    contestar – to answer
visitar – to visit
deber – to ought (should)
quedarse – to stay / to remain
lastimarse – to get hurt / to hurt oneself
soplarse la nariz – to blow one's nose
mejorarse – to get better
empeorarse – to get worse
tomar – to take / to drink
    la pastilla / la píldora – pill
    la medicina – medicine
    el agua (*femenino*) – water

otras palabras y expresiones útiles

Lo siento. – I am sorry. / I feel (bad for)
               what you are going through.
para + *infinitivo* – in order *to* _____
sólo / solamente / nomás – only (*adverb*)
único/a – only (*adjective*)
    la única cita – the only appointment
cada – each / every
también – also
tampoco – either / neither
pero – but
porque – because
por eso – that's why
mucho – a lot / much (*adverb*)
más – more / else (¿Qué más? – What else?)
si – if / whether (no accent mark)

Unidad 11 – la ciudad

los lugares – places
la avenida – avenue
el banco – bank
la biblioteca – library
la calle – street
el cine – movie theater
la cuadra / la manzana – (city) block
la dulcería – candy shop
la esquina – corner
la estación – station
    de policía – police station
    de tren – train station
el estadio – stadium
la farmacia – pharmacy
el hotel – hotel
la iglesia – church
la librería – bookstore
la mezquita – mosque
el monumento – monument
la oficina de correos – post office
la parada de autobús – bus stop
el parque – park
la plaza – plaza
el restaurante – restaurant
la sinagoga – synagogue
el supermercado (súper) – supermarket
el teatro – theater
el templo – temple
la tienda – store / shop
el zoológico (zoo) – zoo
el zócalo / la plaza mayor – town square

las actividades
abrir – to open
    estar abierto/a – to be open
cerrar (e → ie) – to close
    estar cerrado/a – to be closed
sacar un libro – to check out a book
devolver (o → ue) un libro – to return a book
buscar – to look for
encontrar (o → ue) – to find
ir a pasear – to go for a walk
llegar (a) – to arrive (at) / to get (to)
recoger – to pick up
trabajar / chambear – to work
vender – to sell
la comunidad – community
el partido de + *sport* – _____ game
la película (peli) – movie
la obra de teatro – (theatrical) play

las compras – shopping
la bolsa – bag
la caja – box / cash register
el / la cajero/a – cashier / bank teller
el / la cliente/a – customer / client
los comestibles / los abarrotes – groceries
el / la consumidor/a – consumer
consumir – to consume
el consumismo – consumerism
el champú, *pl.* los champúes – shampoo(s)
el cepillo – brush
el cepillo de dientes – toothbrush
el desodorante – deodorant
el dulce – candy
el hilo dental – dental floss
el jabón – soap
la marca – brand
la pasta dentífrica/dental – toothpaste
el peine – comb
el regalo – gift

el dinero – money
el salario / el sueldo – salary
ganar – to earn
gastar – to spend
ahorrar – to save
el cajero automático – ATM
el NIP (número de identificación personal) – PIN
la cuenta – account
    corriente / de cheques – checking account
    de ahorros – savings account
retirar / sacar – to withdraw / to take out
depositar – to deposit
cobrar – to charge
el cargo adicional – additional charge
la comisión – commission / fee
el cambio – change
el recibo / el comprobante – receipt (of purchase)
el saldo / el balance (de cuenta) – (account) balance
el costo – cost
costar (o → ue) – to cost

el transporte – transportation
a pie – on foot
en + *vehicle* – by _____
tomar / coger (un taxi) – to take / to catch (a cab)
el autobús (bus) – bus
el metro – subway
el taxi – taxi(cab)
el tren – train

el correo – mail
la carta – letter
el correo electrónico – email
enviar (i → í) / mandar – to send
la estampilla / el timbre / el sello – stamp
el paquete – package
recibir – to receive
el sobre – envelope
la tarjeta de cumpleaños – birthday card
la (tarjeta) postal – postcard

las direcciones – directions
a – to / away
¿a cuántas cuadras de _____?
　– how many blocks (away) from _____?
a cinco cuadras (de __) – 5 blocks away (from __)
al lado (de) – next to / to the side (of)
el lado – side
cerca (de) – near / close (to)
lejos (de) – far away (from)
arriba – up / above
abajo – down / below
a la vuelta – around the corner
adelante – ahead
atrás – back
detrás (de) – behind
enfrente (de) – across (from) / in front (of)
delante (de) – ahead (of) / in front (of)
entre – between / among
dobla a la izquierda – turn left
　　a la derecha – turn right
sigue derecho – go straight
para / hacia – toward
quedar – to be located
¿Me puede(s) decir en dónde queda _____?
　– Can you tell me where _____ is located?
¿Me puede(s) decir cómo llegar a _____?
　– Can you tell me how to get to _____?

la rutina – routine
a menudo – often
a veces – sometimes
(casi) siempre – (almost) always
(casi) nunca – (almost) never
de vez en cuando – from time to time
frecuentemente – frequently
constantemente – constantly
normalmente – normally
generalmente – generally
en general / por lo general – in general
muchas veces – many times
pocas veces – not very often
raras veces / rara vez – rarely

past activities
hacer: (yo) hice – I did
　　　(tú) hiciste – you did
ir: (yo) fui – I went
　　(tú) fuiste – you went
ver: (yo) vi – I saw
　　(tú) viste – you saw
siguiente – following
　　al día siguiente – the following day
　　a la semana siguiente – the following week
anterior – previous
　　la noche anterior – the previous night
anoche – last night
anteayer / antier – the day before yesterday
anteanoche – the night before last
ayer – yesterday
una vez – once / one time
dos veces – twice / two times
la última vez (que) – the last time (that)
la única vez (que) – the only time (that)
pasado/a – last / past
　　el lunes pasado – last Monday
　　la semana pasada – last week
　　el fin de semana pasado – last weekend
hace + *tiempo* – _____ ago
　　hace 3 años – 3 years ago
luego / más tarde – later
antes (de) – before
después (de) / luego (de) – after / afterward(s)
tarde – late
temprano – early
pronto – soon

otras palabras y frases útiles
¿Qué onda? – What's up?
¿Qué hay (de nuevo)? – What's new?
　　Nada en especial. / No mucho. – Not much.
para – for (intended recipient)
para + *infinitivo* – in order *to* _____
empujar – to push
jalar / halar – to pull
crear – to create
el producto – product
los bienes – goods
los servicios – services
cambiar – to change / to exchange
la opción, *pl.* las opciones – option(s)
quizá(s) / a lo mejor – maybe
la capital – capital (of a city, state, country)

Unidad 12 (parte 1) – la vida escolar

las materias / las asignaturas – subjects
el alemán – German
el álgebra (*femenino*) – algebra
el arte (*masc.*), *pl.* las artes (*fem.*) – art, (the) arts
la banda – band
la biología – biology
el cálculo – calculus
el chino – Chinese
las ciencias – science(s)
el coro – choir
la clase de _____ – _____ class
la educación física – physical education
el español – Spanish
la física – physics
el francés – French
la geografía – geography
la geometría – geometry
la historia – history
el inglés – English
el idioma (*masculino*) / la lengua – language
el japonés – Japanese
la literatura – literature
   la novela – novel
las matemáticas – math
la música – music
la orquesta – orchestra
la química – chemistry
la tecnología – technology
difícil – difficult / hard
fácil – easy
la tarea – homework / task

los materiales escolares – school supplies
la agenda – daily planner
el armario / el casillero / el lóquer – locker
la bandera – flag
el borrador – eraser
la calculadora – calculator
la computadora / el ordenador – computer
el cuaderno – notebook
el diccionario – dictionary
la engrapadora / la grapadora – stapler
el escritorio – desk
el horario – schedule
el lápiz, *pl.* los lápices – pencil(s)
el libro – book
el mapa (*masculino*) – map
el marcador – marker
   de borrado seco – dry-erase marker
la mochila – backpack
el papel – paper

el pizarrón – whiteboard
la pluma / el bolígrafo – pen
el proyector – projector
el pupitre – student desk
el reloj – clock / watch
el (los) sacapuntas – pencil sharpener(s)
la silla – chair
el (los) sujetapapeles – paper clip(s)
la transparencia – transparency

las actividades extracurriculares
el anuario – yearbook
el club, *pl.* los clubs – club(s)
cuidar niños – to babysit
el equipo – team / equipment
el / la miembro (de) – member (of)
participar – to participate
el periódico – (the) newspaper
practicar deportes – to play sports
la reunión – meeting
tocar un instrumento – to play an instrument
trabajar como voluntario/a – to volunteer
el / la tutor/a – tutor

las personas – people / persons
el / la asistente/a – assistant / aide
el / la compañero/a de clase – classmate
el / la consejero/a – counselor
el / la director/a – principal
el / la enfermero/a – nurse
el / la estudiante – student
el / la maestro/a / docente – teacher
el / la secretario/a – secretary
la Sra., la Srta., el Sr. – Mrs., Miss, Mr.

los lugares – places
el ala (*femenino*), *pl.* las alas – wing(s)
el auditorio – auditorium
la biblioteca – library
la cafetería – cafeteria
el edificio – building
el escenario – stage
el gimnasio – gymnasium (gym)
el laboratorio – laboratory
la oficina – office
   de asistencia – attendance office
el piso – floor
el salón de clase / el aula (*femenino*) – classroom
el suelo – ground
el teatro – theater
la universidad (uni) – (the) university / college

¿Cuándo?

temprano – early
a tiempo – on time
tarde – late
antes (de) – before
después (de) – after / afterwards
durante – during
el período / el periodo – period (of time)
el bloque – block
el cuarto – quarter
el semestre – semester
el año – year
escolar – school (*adjective*)
pasado/a – last / past
próximo/a – next
anterior – previous
siguiente – following
empezar (e → ie) – to start / to begin
terminar – to end / to finish
en/por la mañana – in the morning
en/por la tarde – in the afternoon
en/por la noche – at night

la hora – time (of day) / hour

¿A qué hora _____? – At what time _____?
  A la una, a las dos, etc. – At one o'clock, etc.
    y cuarto – quarter past the hour
    y media – half past the hour
  A la una (y) cuarenta y cinco – At 1:45
  A las cuatro (y) quince – At 4:15
de la mañana – in the morning
de la tarde – in the afternoon
de la noche – at night
en punto – on the dot
primero/a (1º / 1ª) – first (1st)
  el primer cuarto (*masculino, singular*)
segundo/a (2º / 2ª) – second (2nd)
tercero/a (3º / 3ª) – third (3rd)
  el tercer cuarto (*masculino, singular*)
cuarto/a (4º / 4ª) – fourth (4th)
quinto/a (5º / 5ª) – fifth (5th)
sexto/a (6º / 6ª) – sixth (6th)
séptimo/a (7º / 7ª) – seventh (7th)
octavo/a (8º / 8ª) – eighth (8th)
noveno/a (9º / 9ª) – ninth (9th)
décimo/a (10º / 10ª) – tenth (10th)
último/a – last / final
el minuto – minute
el segundo – second
el momento – moment
el rato – a small amount of time (a bit)
  Te veo al rato. – I'll see you in a bit.

las acciones

aprender – to learn
conocer (c → zc) – to know (personally)
contestar / responder – to answer
devolver (o → ue) – to return (an item)
enseñar – to teach
entregar – to turn in / to hand in
escribir – to write
estudiar – to study
hablar – to speak / to talk
hacer (una presentación) – to do (a presentation)
hacer una pregunta – to ask a question
hacer fila / hacer cola – to line up / to form a line
jugar (u → ue) – to play
leer – to read
llegar – to arrive
necesitar – to need
repartir – to pass out / to hand out / to distribute
saber (yo sé) – to know (information, facts)
sacar buenas notas – to get good grades
sacar malas notas – to get bad grades
sacar una (foto)copia – to make a (photo)copy
salir (de) – to leave / to go out (from)
tomar/presentar un examen – to take a test
tomar apuntes / sacar apuntes – to take notes
traer – to bring
usar – to use
se permite + *infinitivo* – _____ing is permitted
se prohíbe + *infinitivo* – _____ing is prohibited

otras palabras útiles

la actividad – activity
el capítulo – chapter
la composición – composition
la copia (maestra) – (master) copy
el ejercicio – exercise
el ensayo – essay
la escritura – writing
el examen / la prueba – test / quiz
el informe / el reportaje – report
la lección – lesson
la lectura – reading
la página – page
el párrafo – paragraph
la pregunta – question
el problema (*masculino*) – problem
el proyecto – project
requerir (e → ie) (e → i) – to require
el requisito – requirement
la respuesta – answer / response
la rúbrica / la directriz – rubric
la unidad – unit

Unidad 12 (parte 2) – la vida profesional

los títulos profesionales – professional titles

el / la abogado/a – lawyer / attorney

el / la arquitecto/a – architect

el / la médico/a – medical doctor

    el / la pediatra – pediatrician

    el / la gineco-obstetra – OB/GYN

    el / la cirujano/a – surgeon

    el / la anestesiólogo/a – anesthesiologist

    el / la oftalmólogo/a – ophthalmologist

el / la optometrista – optometrist

el / la ortodoncista – orthodontist

el / la dentista / odontólogo/a – dentist

el / la quiropráctico/a – chiropractor

el / la terapeuta / terapista – therapist

el / la masajista – massage therapist

el / la nutricionista / dietista – nutritionist / dietitian

el / la enfermero/a – nurse

el / la veterinario/a – veterinarian

el / la psiquiatra – psychiatrist

el / la psicólogo/a – psychologist

el / la consejero/a – counselor / advisor

    de finanzas – financial advisor

el / la científico/a – scientist

el / la antropólogo/a – anthropologist

el / la biólogo/a – biologist

el / la bioquímico/a – biochemist

el / la químico/a – chemist

el / la farmacéutico/a / farmaceuta – pharmacist

el / la físico/a – physicist

el / la arqueólogo/a – archeologist

el / la gerente/a – manager

el / la supervisor/a – supervisor

el / la jefe/a – boss

el / la dueño/a – owner

el / la secretario/a – secretary

el / la recepcionista – receptionist

el / la asistente/a – assistant

    de oficina – office assistant

    médico/a – medical assistant

el / la administrador/a – administrator

el / la ingeniero/a – engineer

    eléctrico/a – electrical engineer

    mecánico/a – mechanical engineer

el / la matemático/a – mathematician

el / la estadístico/a – statistician

el / la actuario/a de seguros – actuary

el / la economista – economist

el / la contador/a – accountant

el / la analista – analyst

el / la programador/a – programmer

el campo – field

el derecho – law

la arquitectura – architecture

la medicina – medicine

    la pediatría – pediatrics

    la ginecología-la obstetricia – too long ☺

    la cirugía – surgery

    la anestesia – anesthesia

    la oftalmología – ophthalmology

la optometría – optometry

la ortodoncia – orthodontia

la odontología – dentistry

la quiropráctica – chiropractic

la terapia – therapy

el masaje – massage

la nutrición – nutrition

la enfermería – nursing

la veterinaria – veterinary medicine

la psiquiatría – psychiatry

la psicología – psychology

la consejería – counseling

    de finanzas – financial counseling

las ciencias – science(s)

la antropología – anthropology

la biología – biology

la bioquímica – biochemistry

la química – chemistry

la farmacología – pharmacology

la física – physics

la arqueología – archeology

la gestión – management

la supervisión – supervision

la jefatura / el liderazgo – leadership

la propiedad – ownership / property

la secretaría – secretariat

la recepción – reception

la asistencia – assistance

la administración – administration

la ingeniería – engineering

    eléctrica – electrical engineering

    mecánica – mechanical engineering

las matemáticas – mathematics

la estadística – statistics

el análisis de riesgos – risk analysis

la economía – economy

la contabilidad – accounting

el análisis – analysis

la programación – programming

el / la investigador/a – investigator
el / la policía (poli) – police officer
el / la detective – detective
   privado/a – private detective
el / la diseñador/a – designer
   gráfico/a – graphic designer
   (de) web – web (www.) designer
el / la desarrollador/a – developer
   de aplicaciones – app developer
   de software – software developer
el / la técnico/a – technician
el / la informático/a – computer expert
el / la tecnólogo/a – tech expert
   en sistemas (de información) – IT tech
el / la traductor/a – translator (written)
el / la intérprete – interpreter (verbal)
el / la lingüista – linguist
el / la artista – artist
el / la músico/a – musician
el actor / la actriz – actor / actress
el / la cantante – singer
el / la cantautor/a – singer-songwriter
el / la escritor/a – writer
el / la autor/a – author
el / la poeta – poet
el / la pintor/a – painter
el / la modelo – model
el / la periodista – journalist
el / la plomero/a – plumber
el / la contratista – contractor
el / la electricista – electrician
el / la mecánico/a – mechanic
   de automóviles (autos) – auto mechanic
el / la jardinero/a – gardener / landscaper
el / la conserje – janitor / custodian
el / la obrero/a – laborer (usually manual)
el / la trabajador/a – worker (any)
el / la empleado/a – employee
el / la especialista – specialist
el / la cajero/a – cashier / bank teller
el / la emprendedor/a – entrepreneur
el / la mesero/a – waiter / waitress
el / la cocinero/a – cook / chef
el / la experto/a / perito/a – expert
el / la agente – agent
el / la empresario/a – business man/woman
el / la vendedor/a – salesperson
el / la estético/a – esthetician / beautician
el / la peluquero/a – barber / hairdresser
el departamento de ____ – ____ department
   recursos humanos – human resources dept.
   servicio al cliente – customer service dept.

la investigación – research / investigation
la policía (poli) – (the) police / policing
las investigaciones reservadas – investigation

el diseño – design
   gráfico – graphic design
   (de) web – web design
el desarrollo – development
   de aplicaciones – app development
   de software – software development

la informática / la computación – computing
la tecnología – technology
   en sistemas (de información) – IT
la traducción – translation (written)
la interpretación – interpretation (verbal)
la lingüística – linguistics
el arte (*masc.*), *pl.* las artes (*fem.*) – art, (the) arts
la música – music
el cine (cinema), el teatro, la televisión, etc.
la música – music

la escritura – writing
la literatura – literature
la poesía – poetry
la pintura – painting
la moda – fashion
el periodismo – journalism
la plomería – plumbing
la contratación – contracting
la electricidad – electricity
la mecánica – mechanics
   de automóviles (autos) – auto mechanics
la jardinería – gardening / landscaping
la limpieza – cleaning
la obra / la labor – labor
el trabajo / la chamba – work / job
el empleo – employment
la especialidad – specialty
la caja – cash register
(trabajar) por cuenta propia – self-employed
el servicio – service
la gastronomía – gastronomy
la pericia – expertise
la agencia – agency
los negocios – business
las ventas – sales
la estética – esthetics / beauty
la peluquería – hairdressing

el personal – personnel

otras personas y organizaciones – other people and organizations

el / la cliente/a – client / customer
el / la oficial – official
el club rotario – rotary club
la ONG (organización no gubernamental) – NGO (non-governmental organization)
sin fines de lucro – not-for-profit / non-profit
la empresa – business / company
la sociedad anónima (S. A.) – corporation (Inc.)
el gobierno – (the) government
   federal – federal
   estatal – state
   municipal – city / municipal

el / la colega – colleague
el / la socio/a – associate / partner
trabajar como voluntario/a – to volunteer

rentable – profitable
la compañía – large company

gubernamental – governmental
el país – (the) country
el estado – (the) state
la ciudad – (the) city
el condado – (the) county

los materiales de oficina – office supplies

la agenda – daily planner
el bloc de notas – notepad
el borrador – eraser
la calculadora – calculator
la cinta adhesiva – adhesive tape
la computadora / el ordenador – computer
el cuaderno – notebook
el documento – document
la engrapadora / la grapadora – stapler
el escritorio – desk
la fotocopiadora – photocopier
el horario – schedule
la impresora – printer
el lápiz, *pl.* los lápices – pencil(s)
el maletín, *pl.* los maletines – briefcase(s)
la máquina de fax – fax machine
el marcador – marker
el pizarrón – whiteboard
la pluma / el bolígrafo – pen
el proyector – projector
el reloj – clock / watch
el (los) sacapuntas – pencil sharpener(s)
la silla – chair
el (los) sujetapapeles – paper clip(s)
la transparencia – transparency

los idiomas más comunes

el alemán – German
el árabe – Arabic
el bengalí – Bengali
el chino – Chinese
   el mandarín – Mandarin
   el cantonés – Cantonese
el español – Spanish
el francés – French
el hindi – Hindi
el inglés – English
el italiano – Italian
el japonés – Japanese
el portugués – Portuguese
el ruso – Russian
la lengua de signos/señas – sign language
el lenguaje corporal – body language

otras palabras y frases útiles

dedicarse (a) – to dedicate oneself (to)
¿A qué te dedicas? – What do you do for work?
   Me dedico a la ingeniería. / Soy ingeniera.
(la) oferta y (la) demanda – supply and demand
el salón de _____ – _____ room
   descanso – break room
   conferencias – conference room
renunciar (a) – to quit (a job)
tomar una decisión – to make a decision
el currículum / la hoja de vida – résumé / CV
la entrevista – interview
las prestaciones – employment benefits
la base de datos – database
el cubículo – cubicle
el tiempo / el plazo – time
el puesto / la plaza – position
   de tiempo completo – full-time position
   de tiempo parcial – part-time position
¡Gusto en verte! – Nice to see you!

la hora – time (of day) / hour

¿A qué hora _____? – At what time _____?
   A la una, a las dos, etc. – At one o'clock, etc.
      y cuarto – quarter past the hour
      y media – half past the hour
   A la una (y) cuarenta y cinco – At 1:45
   A las cuatro (y) quince – At 4:15
de la mañana – in the morning
de la tarde – in the afternoon
de la noche – at night

Unidad 13 – la rutina diaria

la rutina diaria – daily routine
acostarse (o → ue) – to lie down
afeitarse / rasurarse (las piernas) – to shave
almorzar (o → ue) – to eat lunch
amarrarse los zapatos – to tie one's shoes
bañarse – to take a bath
cenar – to eat dinner
cepillarse (el pelo, los dientes) – to brush
desayunar – to eat breakfast
el despertador – alarm clock
despertarse (e → ie) – to wake up
    estar despierto/a – to be awake
dormir (o → ue) (o → u) – to sleep
    roncar – to snore
dormirse (o → ue) (o → u) – to fall asleep
    estar dormido/a – to be asleep
ducharse – to shower
la higiene – hygiene
irse (de) / marcharse (de) – to leave (from)
lavarse (la cara, las manos, los dientes)
    – to wash one's _____
levantarse – to get up
maquillarse – to put on makeup
    desmaquillarse – to take off one's makeup
peinarse (el pelo) – to comb
prepararse / alistarse (para) – to get ready (for)
regresar – to return
salir (de) – to leave / to go out (from)
secarse (el pelo, el cuerpo) – to dry one's _____
soler (o → ue) + *inf.* – to be in the habit of __*ing*
vestirse (e → i) (e → i) (de) – to get dressed
    desvestirse – to get undressed

la música – music
la banda – band
tocar – to play (an instrument)
la canción – song
cantar – to sing
el coro – choir / chorus
la orquesta – orchestra
el instrumento musical – musical instrument
    el clarinete – clarinet
    el contrabajo – upright bass / double bass
    la flauta – flute
    el piano – piano
    el saxofón – saxophone
    el tambor – drum
        la batería – drums (drum kit)
    la trompeta – trumpet
    el violín – violin

las actividades extracurriculares
participar (en) – to participate (in)
el anuario – yearbook
las artes marciales – martial arts
el club, *pl.* los clubs – club(s)
el consejo estudiantil – student council
cuidar niños – to babysit
los deportes – sports
    el atletismo – track and field
    el béisbol – baseball
    el hockey – hockey
    el sófbol – softball
    el fútbol – soccer
    el fútbol americano – football
    el básquetbol – basketball
    el voleibol – volleyball
    la natación – swimming
    el golf – golf
entrenar – to train
el equipo (de _____) – (_____) team
jugar (u → ue) – to play (a sport, a game)
levantar pesas – to lift weights
montar en bicicleta (bici) – to ride a bicycle
nadar – to swim
practicar – to practice
el periódico (de la escuela) – newspaper
repartir – to pass out / to hand out
ser miembro (de) – to be a member (of)
trabajar como voluntario/a – to volunteer
el / la tutor/a – tutor
agarrar / coger – to grab

la hora – time (of day) / hour
¿A qué hora? – At what time?
a las siete (y) cincuenta – At 7:50
al diez para las ocho – At 7:50
a las ocho menos diez – At 7:50
a eso de las ocho – at about 8:00
alrededor de las ocho – at around 8:00
como a las ocho – like at 8:00
y media – :30
y cuarto – :15
menos cuarto – 15 minutes to the hour
antes de + *infinitivo* – before _____*ing*
después de + *infinitivo* – after _____*ing*
durante – during
mientras – while
el momento – moment
a la vez / al mismo tiempo – at the same time

palabras de acción habitual (el presente)
(casi) siempre – (almost) always
(casi) nunca – (almost) never
(casi) todos los días – (almost) every day
(casi) todo el tiempo – (almost) all the time
a veces – sometimes
muchas veces – many times
a menudo – often
de vez en cuando – from time to time
constantemente – constantly
normalmente – normally
usualmente – usually
frecuentemente – frequently
generalmente – generally
por lo general – in general / generally
en general – in general
los lunes – (on) Mondays
los fines de semana – (on) the weekends
cada sábado – each Saturday / every Saturday
cada día – each day / every day

palabras claves que indican el pretérito
anoche – last night
anteayer / antier – the day before yesterday
anteanoche – the night before last
ayer – yesterday
siguiente – following
    al día siguiente – the following day
    a la semana siguiente – the following week
anterior – previous
    la noche anterior – the previous night
una vez – once / one time
dos veces – twice / two times
la última vez (que) – the last time (that)
la única vez (que) – the only time (that)
hace + *tiempo* – _____ ago
    hace 3 semanas – 3 weeks ago
    hace 4 años – 4 years ago
pasado/a – last / past
    el miércoles pasado – last Wednesday
    la semana pasada – last week
    el fin de semana pasado – last weekend
luego / más tarde – later
antes (de) – before
después (de) / luego (de) – after / afterward(s)
tarde – late
temprano – early
pronto – soon

otras palabras y expresiones útiles
tener que ver (con) – to have to do (with)
depender (de) – to depend (on)
    depende del día – depends on the day
estar de buen humor – to be in a good mood
estar de mal humor – to be in a bad mood
pero – but
porque – because
    Llegué tarde porque salí de casa tarde.
como – since / given that (to start a sentence)
    Como salí de casa tarde, llegué tarde.
mismo/a – same
por lo menos – at least
con – with
sin – without
sin + *infinitivo* – without _____ing
el secador – hair dryer
la toalla – towel
final – final
el final – (the) end
al final – at the end

Unidad 14 – la ropa

las prendas de vestir – articles of clothing
el abrigo – coat
la bata – bathrobe
la blusa – blouse
la bolsa – purse / bag
las botas – boots
la bufanda – scarf
el calcetín, *pl.* los calcetines – sock(s)
la camisa – shirt
la camiseta – T-shirt
la cartera – wallet
el chaleco – vest
    salvavidas – life vest / life jacket
la chamarra / la chaqueta – jacket
las chanclas / las sandalias – sandals
el cinturón / el cinto – belt
    la hebilla – buckle
la corbata – tie / necktie
el esmoquin – tuxedo
la falda – skirt
la gorra / la cachucha – hat (with visor) / ball cap
el gorro – hat (without visor)
los guantes – gloves
los jeans – jeans (pronounced as in English)
la joyería – jewelry / jewelry store
    el anillo – ring
    el arete / el pendiente – earring
    el brazalete / la pulsera – bracelet
    el collar – necklace
las manoplas – mittens
los mocasines – dress shoes / loafers
los pantalones – pants
    los (pantalones) cortos – shorts
    deportivos – sweatpants / athletic pants
las pantuflas – slippers
el pañuelo – handkerchief
el pijama / la piyama – pajamas
la ropa – clothing / clothes
el saco – sports jacket (suit jacket)
el sombrero – hat (with full brim)
la (camisa) sudadera – sweatshirt
el suéter – sweater
    de cuello alto – turtle-neck sweater
el traje – suit
el traje de baño / el bañador – bathing suit
el vestido – dress
los zapatos – shoes
    de tacón alto – high-heel shoes
los (zapatos de) tenis – tennis shoes

las partes de la ropa
el bolsillo – pocket
el botón – button
la capucha – hood
el cierre – zipper
la costura – seam
el cuello – collar
la manga (corta, larga) – (short, long) sleeve

las descripciones
apretado/a / ajustado/a – tight
cómodo/a – comfortable
corto/a – short
elegante – elegant / fancy / formal
flojo/a / suelto/a – baggy / loose
incómodo/a – uncomfortable
largo/a – long
sencillo/a – simple / casual / every-day
estar de moda – to be in fashion/style
llevar / portar – to carry
llevar (puesto/a) – to wear (clarifies ambiguity)
ponerse – to put on (oneself)
probarse (o → ue) – to try on (oneself)
quitarse – to take off (oneself)
usar – to use / to wear (a specific size)
verse – to look (as in, "How do I look?")
vestirse (e → i) (e → i) (de) – to get dressed

los comparativos – comparatives
más + *adjetivo* + que – more _____ than
menos + *adjetivo* + que – less _____ than
mejor que – better than
peor que – worse than
tan + *adjetivo* + como – as _____ as

sizes
el número (de zapatos) – size (in numbers)
la etiqueta – tag / label
la talla – size (official size from a tag)
    extra grande (XG) – extra large
    grande (G) – large
    mediana (M) – medium
    chica (C) – small
    extra chica (XC) – extra small
    unitalla – one size fits all
el tamaño – size (general – house, cat, etc.)
grande – large
mediano/a – medium
pequeño/a – small

fabrics, patterns, colors
la tela / el tejido – fabric
el algodón – cotton
el cuero / la piel – leather / hide
la lana – wool
la lona – canvas
la mezclilla – denim
el nilón – nylon
la pana – corduroy
el plástico – plastic
el poliéster – polyester
el rayón – rayon
la seda – silk
sintético/a – synthetic
el diseño / el patrón – design / pattern
de cuadros – checkered / plaid
de rayas – striped
floreado/a – floral / flowery
liso/a – straight / smooth / plain
¿De qué es _____? – What is _____ made of?
   Es de _____. – It's made of _____.
¿De qué color es _____? – What color is _____?
   La camisa es morada claro. (*claro* modifies *color*)
   La camisa es de un color morado oscuro.

de compras
el / la cajero/a – cashier
el / la vendedor/a – salesperson
el catálogo – catalog
el producto – product
desear – to desire / to want
buscar – to look for
encontrar (o → ue) – to find
escoger – to choose
costar (o → ue) – to cost
comprar – to buy / to purchase
vender – to sell
pagar – to pay (for)
devolver (o → ue) – to return (an item)
el cheque – check
(el dinero en) efectivo – cash (money)
la tarjeta de crédito (débito) – credit (debit) card
barato/a (una ganga) – cheap (a bargain)
caro/a (un robo) – expensive (a ripoff)
nuevo/a – new
de segunda mano (usado/a) – second-hand (used)
la tienda de segunda mano – second-hand store
la liquidación – clearance / liquidation
estar en liquidación – to be on clearance
la tienda de descuentos – discount store
el descuento / la rebaja – sale
estar de descuento/rebaja – to be on sale

la tienda de ropa – clothing store
la zapatería – shoe store
para mí, ti, ella, nosotros – for me, you, her, us
por 30 dólares – for 30 dollars
el / la costurero/a – seamster / seamstress
el / la sastre/a – tailor (mainly for men's clothing)
sin compromiso – without any commitment (to buy)

los adjetivos demostrativos – demonstrative adj.
este (*masc.*) / esta (*fem.*) / esto (*neutro*) – this
estos / estas – these
ese / esa / eso – that (nearer than *aquel*)
esos / esas – those
aquel / aquella / aquello – that (farther than *ese*)
aquellos / aquellas – those

el clima (*masculino*) / el tiempo – the weather
hace (mucho) calor – it's (really) hot
hace (mucho) frío – it's (really) cold
hace (mucho) viento – it's (really) windy
hace (mucho) sol – it's (really) sunny
hace (muy) buen tiempo – it's (very) nice out
está (muy) nublado – it's (very) cloudy
llover (o → ue) (la lluvia) – to rain
nevar (e → ie) (la nieve) – to snow
lloviznar (la llovizna) – to drizzle
granizar (el granizo) – to hail
la tormenta – storm

otras palabras y expresiones útiles
parecer (c → zc) – to seem (like)
¿Qué te parece? – What do you think (of it)?
   Me parece bien. – It seems fine.
   Me parece flojo/a. – It seems loose.
quedar – to fit
¿Cómo te queda? – How does it fit you?
   Me queda bien. – It fits fine.
   Me queda un poco flojo/a. – It fits a little loose.
el cesto de la ropa sucia – dirty-clothes hamper
el piso / el suelo – floor / ground
la fiesta / la pachanga / el reventón – party / blowout
colgar (o → ue) – to hang (up)
guardar – to put away / to keep
otro/a – other / another
¡Qué + *adjetivo*! – How _____!
alguien – someone
nadie – no one
   – anyone (in a negative sentence)
todo el mundo – everyone
por todas partes – everywhere
la parte superior – the top (part)
la parte inferior – the bottom (part)

Unidad 15 – la alimentación y los restaurantes

los alimentos y las bebidas – food and drinks

el aceite de oliva – olive oil
el aderezo – salad dressing (thick)
el agua embotellada – bottled water
el agua purificada – purified water
el aliño – salad dressing (vinegar, oil)
el arroz – rice
la avena – oats
el (la) azúcar – sugar
el bistec – steak
la carne de res – beef
el cerdo / el puerco – pork / pig
el chile – spicy pepper (sauce)
el chorizo – a type of spicy sausage
la crema – sour cream / whipped cream
la ensalada (de) – salad
las especias – spices
el frijol (pinto, negro) – (pinto, black) bean
la fruta – fruit
el helado / la nieve – ice cream
el hielo – ice
el huevo – egg
el jugo / el zumo – juice
la leche – milk
el licuado / el batido – smoothie
el marisco – shellfish
la paleta – popsicle
el pastel / la torta / la tarta – cake
el pescado – fish (prepared)
el pollo – chicken
el postre – dessert
el maíz / el elote – corn
el pan – bread
la papa / la patata – potato
la papita – potato chip
el pimiento – (bell) pepper
el queso (rallado) – (shredded) cheese
el refresco / la soda / la gaseosa – soft drink
la sal y la pimienta – salt and (black) pepper
la salchicha – sausage / hot dog
la salsa (picante) – (hot) sauce
la sazón, *pl.* las sazones – seasoning(s)
la sopa / el caldo (de) – soup / broth
la tapa / el antojito – finger food
el tocino – bacon
la tortilla de harina – flour tortilla
la tortilla de maíz – corn tortilla
la tortilla dorada – taco shell
la tortilla española (de patatas) – like a quiche
el totopo – tortilla chip
el trigo – wheat

las descripciones y las acciones

algo – something
asqueroso/a – disgusting / gross
    ¡Qué asco! / ¡Guácala! – Yuck!
beber / tomar – to drink
bravo/a – very spicy (hot)
bueno/a – good
caliente – hot (temperature)
chupar – to suck
crujiente / crispi – crunchy / crispy
delicioso/a / rico/a – delicious
dulce – sweet
engullir – to gobble down / to gulp down
eructar – to burp
escupir – to spit
estar – to be (based on your experience)
frío/a – cold
grasoso/a – fatty
    la grasa – fat / grease
incluir (y) – to include
lamer / lamber – to lick
malo/a – bad
masticar – to chew
merendar (e → ie) – to snack at midday
la merienda – afternoon snack
mismo/a – same
morder (o → ue) – to bite
    la mordida / el mordisco – bite
oler (o → hue) – to smell
    huele(n) (a) – smell(s) (like)
el olor (a) – smell (of)
el pedazo / el trozo – piece / chunk
picante / picoso/a – spicy (medium)
el plato (principal) – (main) dish
probar (o → ue) – to taste / to try
la ración / la porción – portion / side
saborear – to taste / to savor
sabe(n) (a) – taste(s) (like)
sabroso/a / bueno/a – tasty
salado/a – salty
satisfacer (conjugates like *hacer*) – to satisfy
satisfecho/a / lleno/a – satisfied / full
soso/a / insípido/a – bland
ser – to be (characteristics)
tener (mucha) hambre – to be (really) hungry
    estar hambriento/a – to be hungry
tener (mucha) sed – to be (really) thirsty
    estar sediento/a – to be thirsty
tibio/a – warm
tragar(se) – to swallow
vomitar – to vomit

la preparación – preparation

afilado/a / filoso/a – sharp (blade)
agregar / añadir – to add
asado/a – broiled / grilled / rotisserie
casero/a – homemade
cocinado/a / cocido/a – cooked
cocinar / cocer (o → ue) (c → z) – to cook
con – with
congelado/a – frozen
congelar – to freeze
cortar – to cut
crudo/a – raw
la cucharada – teaspoonful
descongelar – to thaw
echar – to throw on, in, or out
enlatado/a – canned
faltar – to be missing
freír (e → í) (e →) – to fry
fresco/a – fresh
frito/a – fried
fundido/a – melted
hecho/a a mano – made by hand
al horno – baked
hornear – to bake
la lata – can
lavar – to wash
molido/a – ground (up)
la olla – pot
a la parrilla – grilled / barbequed
picar / triturar – to chop (up) / to dice
poner a fuego lento – to let simmer
preparar – to prepare
puntiagudo/a – sharp (point / tip)
quemado/a – burnt / burned
quemar – to burn
relleno/a – stuffed
revuelto/a – scrambled
el (la) sartén – frying pan / skillet
sazonar – to season
sin – without

el tiempo y el espacio (las preposiciones)

alrededor (de) – around
antes (de) – before
debajo (de) – below / underneath
detrás (de) – behind
en – in / on / at
encima (de) / sobre – on top (of)
enfrente (de) / delante (de) – in front (of)
entre – between / among
en seguida – next / immediately following
luego (de) / después (de) – after / afterward(s)

el restaurante – restaurant

a la carta – a la carte (by itself)
el aperitivo / el entremés – appetizer
la caja para llevar – to-go box / doggy bag
los cubiertos – silverware
    la cuchara – spoon
    el cuchillo – knife
    el tenedor – fork
la cuenta – (the) bill / (the) check
dar (yo doy) – to give
derramar – to spill out / to spill over
la especialidad de la casa – house special
llevar – to carry / to take (from here to there)
llevarse – to take with (oneself)
el mantel – tablecloth
el / la mesero/a – server (waiter / waitress)
    el / la camarero/a – server (waiter / waitress)
el menú / la carta – menu
el mostrador – counter
pasar (la sal) – to pass (the salt)
pagar (por) – to pay (for) / to pay for
pagar $30 por _____ – to pay $30 for _____
para llevar – to-go / for carry-out
pedir (e → i) (e → i) – to order / to request
por favor – please
el platillo – saucer
el plato del día – special of the day
el popote / la paja / el pitillo – straw
la propina – tip / gratuity
la servilleta – napkin
servir (e → i) (e → i) – to serve
sobrar – to be too much
las sobras – leftovers
el tamaño – size
la taza – cup
el tazón – bowl
traer – to bring (from there to here)
los trastes / los platos – dishes
el vaso – glass
verter (e → ie) – to pour / to spill

otras palabras y expresiones útiles

Se me hace agua la boca. – It makes my mouth water.
Es para chuparse los dedos. – It's finger-licking good.
Se me antoja(n) _____. – I'm in the mood for _____.
Me apetece(n) ___. – ___ sound(s) appetizing to me.
abrir el apetito – to whet one's appetite
¿Qué hay de comer? – What is there to eat?
¿Qué hay de postre? – What's for dessert?
una mesa para 4 – a table for 4
Yo quisiera ___ / Me gustaría ___ – I would like ___
¿Me pudiera traer _____? – Could you bring me _____?

Unidad 16 – los deportes, los juegos y las diversiones

los deportes – sports
el atletismo – track and field
el básquetbol / el baloncesto – basketball
el béisbol – baseball
el billar – billiards / pool
el boliche – bowling
el ciclismo – cycling
el clavadismo – diving
el cross – cross country
el fútbol (sóquer) – soccer
el fútbol americano – (American) football
la gimnasia – gymnastics
el golf – golf
el hockey – hockey (pronounced as in English)
el lacrosse – lacrosse
la lucha libre – wrestling
la natación – swimming
las porras / la animación – cheerleading
el ráquetbol – racquetball
el rugby – rugby
el sófbol – softball
el voleibol – volleyball

las acciones
anotar un punto/tanto – to score a point
atrapar / cachar – to catch
batear – to bat
calentarse (e → ie) – to warm up / to get warmed up
    el calentamiento – warm-up
competir (e → i) (e → i) – to compete
correr – to run
derrapar – to slide
entrenar – to train / to practice
esquiar (i → í) – to ski
estirarse (los músculos) – to stretch (one's muscles)
    el estiramiento – stretching
hacer clavados – to dive
jugar (u → ue) – to play (sports)
lanzar – to throw / to pitch
levantar pesas – to lift weights
luchar – to fight / to struggle / to wrestle
meter un gol, cesto – to score a goal, basket
montar en bicicleta – to ride a bicycle
nadar – to swim
patear – to kick
patinar sobre hielo, ruedas – to ice, roller skate
pegar / golpear / dar – to hit
practicar – to practice / to play (sports)
sacar la pelota – to serve the ball
saltar / brincar – to jump
tirar – to shoot (basketball, soccer, etc.) / to throw

el equipo – equipment
el balón, *pl.* los balones – (big, inflatable) ball(s)
el bate – bat
la bola (de boliche, de billar) – ball (solid)
la cancha / el campo – court / field
el casco – helmet
el disco de hockey – hockey puck
el esquí, *pl.* los esquíes – ski(s)
el guante (de béisbol) – (baseball) glove
el palo (de golf, de hockey, etc.) – club / stick
el patín, *pl.* los patines – skate(s)
la pelota (de tenis) – (tennis) ball
las pesas – weights
la piscina (pisci) / la alberca – swimming pool
la pista – (race) track / (skating, hockey) rink
la portería – goal (soccer, hockey, etc.)
los protectores – pads
la raqueta (de tenis) – (tennis) racket
la red – net
el tablero – board (diving, chess, etc.)
el uniforme – uniform
los zapatos con clavos / los tacos – cleats

la liga – league
el campeón / la campeona – champion
el campeonato / la final – championship / (the) finals
la competencia – meet / competition
contra – against
la derrota – defeat / loss
derrotar / vencer (c → z) – to defeat
empatar – to tie
el empate – tie
el error – error
ganar – to win / to earn
mundial – world (*adjective*)
el mundo – world
el partido – game / match
el penalti – penalty
perder (e → ie) – to lose
premiar – to award
el premio – prize / award
retar / desafiar (i → í) – to challenge
el reto / el desafío – challenge
la rivalidad – rivalry
la temporada – (sports) season
    la postemporada – postseason / playoffs
el torneo – tournament
el triunfo – triumph
triunfar – to triumph
el trofeo – trophy
la victoria – victory / win

los juegos y las diversiones – fun and games
apostar (o → ue) – to bet
la apuesta – bet
la diversión – fun (*noun*)
(jugar a) el ajedrez – chess
(jugar a) las damas – checkers
(jugar a) las cartas – cards
(jugar a) el juego de mesa – board game
el desfile – parade
la exposición (expo) (de arte) – (art) exhibit
(hacer) un crucigrama (*masc.*) – crossword puzzle
(hacer) un pícnic – picnic
(hacer) un rompecabezas – puzzle
tocar un instrumento – to play an instrument
la obra de teatro – (theatrical) play
ensayar – to rehearse / to try out (for something)
la fiesta de disfraces – costume party
el disfraz, *pl.* los disfraces – costume(s)
la música clásica – classical music
la música rock – rock music
el concierto – concert
(la música) en vivo / en directo – live (music)
el disco compacto / el cidí – compact disc / CD
el archivo de mp3 – mp3 file
el video/vídeo musical – music video
aburrirse – to get bored
divertirse (e → ie) (e → i) – to have fun
pasarlo bien, mal – to have a good, bad time

las personas
el / la árbitro/a – referee / umpire
el / la atleta – athlete
el / la ciclista – cyclist
el / la clavadista – diver
el / la entrenador/a – coach / trainer
el / la fan / hincha / aficionado/a – fan
el / la jugador/a – player
el / la miembro (de) – member (of)
el / la nadador/a – swimmer
el / la porrista / animador/a – cheerleader
el equipo – team

las descripciones
alegre / feliz – happy
chévere / chido/a – cool / sweet / awesome
divertido/a – fun (*adjective*)
estupendo/a – stupendous
genial – cool / brilliant
lento/a – slow
lentamente / despacio – slowly
rápido/a – fast / quick
rápidamente – quickly
lo máximo / la leche – the best/coolest thing

los números ordinales – ordinal numbers
primero/a (1º / 1ª) – first (1st)
    el primer cuarto (*masculino, singular*)
segundo/a (2º / 2ª) – second (2nd)
tercero/a (3º / 3ª) – third (3rd)
    el tercer cuarto (*masculino, singular*)
cuarto/a (4º / 4ª) – fourth (4th)
quinto/a (5º / 5ª) – fifth (5th)
sexto/a (6º / 6ª) – sixth (6th)
séptimo/a (7º / 7ª) – seventh (7th)
octavo/a (8º / 8ª) – eighth (8th)
noveno/a (9º / 9ª) – ninth (9th)
décimo/a (10º / 10ª) – tenth (10th)
último/a – last / final

non-action verbs in the preterite
poder: (yo) pude – I succeeded / managed to
    no pude – I failed to
querer: (yo) quise – I wanted / attempted to
    no quise – I didn't want / I refused to
saber: (yo) supe – I found out
    no supe – I didn't find out
tener: (yo) tuve – I got / received
    no tuve – I didn't get / receive
    (yo) tuve que – I had (was forced) to
    no tuve que – I didn't end up having to

otras palabras y expresiones útiles
Deséame suerte. – Wish me luck.
¡Buena suerte! – Good luck!
¡Qué horror! – How awful! / How terrible!
¡Qué desastre! – What a disaster!
¡Qué bueno/bien! – Good! / Great!
Ándale (pues). – Get to it (then).
¡Ánimo! – Come on! (encouragement) / Cheer up!
¡Échale ganas! – Give it all you got! / Do your best!
al fin de cuentas … – when it was all over …
de todas formas – anyway / anyhow
    de todos modos – anyway / anyhow
    de todas maneras – anyway / anyhow
Te toca a ti. – It's your turn.
Le toca a Mario. – It's Mario's turn.
digo – I mean (self correction)
tener que ver (con) – to have to do (with)
¿Cómo te va? – How is it going for you?
    (Todo) me va bien. – (Everything) is going
        well for me.
¿Cómo te fue? – How did it go for you?
    (Todo) me fue bien. – It (all) went well for me.
bastante – quite / rather (*adverb*), enough (*adjective*)
¡Basta (ya)! – That's enough (already)! / Stop it!
tener tiempo de + *infinitivo* – to have time *to _____*
para + *infinitivo* – in order *to _____*

Unidad 17 – la niñez y la juventud

las descripciones

el niño / el chamaco – boy / child
la niña / la chamaca – girl / child
el / la vecino/a – neighbor
amable – kind / nice
antipático/a – mean
artístico/a – artistic
atrevido/a – daring
callado/a – quiet / not talkative
chistoso/a – funny
codo/a / tacaño/a – cheap / stingy
consentido/a – spoiled
deportista – athletic
desobediente – disobedient
(bien) educado/a – well mannered
egoísta – selfish
flojo/a / perezoso/a – lazy
generoso/a – generous
impaciente – impatient
joven – young
maleducado/a – rude
(hermano) mayor – older (brother)
(hermana) menor – younger (sister)
molesto/a / molestoso/a – annoying
obediente – obedient
paciente – patient
prudente – cautious / careful
simpático/a – nice
sociable – sociable
tímido/a – timid / shy
travieso/a – mischievous
viejo/a – old
demasiado + *adjetivo* – too _____
demasiado/a – too much
la cualidad – quality / characteristic

adonde van los niños

la biblioteca – library
la dulcería – candy store
la librería – book store
el parque – park
asistir (a) – to attend
la guardería infantil – daycare
el preescolar – preschool
el kínder – kindergarten
la escuela primaria – elementary school
la escuela secundaria – middle school
la escuela preparatoria – high school
    (school nomenclature varies by country)

el equipo del patio de recreo

el recreo / el receso – recess
el patio de recreo – playground
el cajón de arena – sandbox
el carrusel – merry-go-round
el columpio – swing
el sube y baja – see-saw / teeter-totter
el tobogán – slide

los juguetes – toys

el animal de peluche – stuffed animal
    el oso de peluche – teddy bear
el bloque – block
el camión – truck
el dinosaurio – dinosaur
el escondite / las escondidas – hide and seek
el juego – game
la muñeca – doll
el muñeco – action figure
el robot, *pl.* los robots – robot(s)
el tren (de juguete) – (toy) train
el regalo – gift / present

las mascotas – pets

el animal – animal
el burro – donkey
el caballo – horse
la cabra – goat
el cangrejo – crab
el cerdo / el cochino – pig
la cobaya / el cuy (cui) – guinea pig
la gallina – hen
el gallo – rooster
el gato – cat
el hámster – hamster
el hurón – ferret
la lagartija – (small) lizard
la llama – llama
la oveja – sheep
el pájaro – bird
el pavo – turkey
el pavo real – peacock
el perro – dog
el pez, *pl.* los peces – fish
el ratón – mouse
la serpiente – snake
la tortuga – turtle
la vaca – cow
la correa – leash

what you used to do (el imperfecto)

ser: (yo) era – I used to be
ir: (tú) ibas – you used to go
ver: (él) veía – he used to see/watch
acompañar – to accompany / to go with
aprender – to learn
bromear (con) – to joke / to kid (around) (with)
caminar – to walk
cantar – to sing
canturrear – to sing softly / to hum
chillar – to scream / to cry
colarse (o → ue) / colearse – to cut in line
la colección – collection
coleccionar – to collect
compartir (con) – to share (with)
el comportamiento – behavior
comportarse / portarse – to behave (oneself)
conocer (c → zc) – to know (personally)
                 – to be familiar with (a place, etc.)
correr – to run
crecer (c → zc) – to grow (up)
decir (yo digo) (e → i) – to say / to tell
desobedecer (c → zc) – to disobey
dibujar – to draw
enojarse (con / de) – to get angry (with, at / from)
escribir – to write
estudiar – to study
extrañar / echar de menos – to miss
fingir – to pretend
gritar – to yell / to shout
hablar en voz alta – to speak out loud / aloud
hablar en voz baja – to speak quietly
hacer un berrinche – to throw a fit/tantrum
jugar (u → ue) – to play
leer – to read
llorar – to cry
    la lágrima – tear
molestar / fastidiar – to annoy / to bother
montar en triciclo – to ride a tricycle
mentir (e → ie) (e → i) – to lie
la mentira – lie
murmurar – to mutter
obedecer (c → zc) – to obey
olvidar – to forget
pelear(se) (con) – to fight (with)
practicar – to practice
quejarse (de) – to complain (about)
la realidad – reality
recordar (o → ue) – to remember
recordar + *infinitivo* – to remember _____ing
recordar (a) – to remind (of)
refunfuñar – to grumble
saber – to know (information, facts)

saber + *infinitivo* – to know how to _____
saltar / brincar (la cuerda/soga) – to jump (rope)
soportar / aguantar – to put up with / to tolerate
susurrar – to whisper
tararear – to hum
tener (e → ie) – to have
la verdad – (the) truth
vivir – to live

la frecuencia de la acción habitual
     (el presente o el imperfecto)
a menudo / muchas veces – often
a veces – sometimes
raras veces / rara vez – rarely
cada – each / every
nunca / jamás – never
               – ever (in a negative sentence)
nunca jamás – never ever
(casi) siempre – (almost) always
cuando – when
de pequeño/a / de niño/a – as a kid / as a child
de vez en cuando – from time to time
constantemente – constantly
frecuentemente – frequently
típicamente – typically
generalmente – generally
normalmente – normally
(casi) todos los días – (almost) every day
todos los viernes – every Friday

otras palabras y expresiones útiles
castigar – to punish
regañar – to scold / to reprimand
hay – there is / there are
había – there was / there were
diferente / distinto/a – different / distinct
mismo/a – same
igual (que) – the same (as)
pero – but
por eso – that's why / for that
porque – because
más + *adjetivo* + que – more _____ than
menos + *adjetivo* + que – less _____ than
tan + *adjetivo* + como – as _____ as
de (posesión) – of (there is no apostrophe)
    el gato de mi mamá – my mom's cat
alguno/a(s) – some
    algún – some (before *singular, masculine noun*)
ninguno/a – none (effectively no *plural* form)
               – any (in a negative sentence)
    ningún – no (before *singular, masculine noun*)
               – any (in a negative sentence)
unos / unas – some

Unidad 18 – la familia y las celebraciones

los familiares – family members
el abuelo – grandfather
el abuelito – grandpa
la abuela – grandmother
la abuelita – grandma
el bisabuelo – great grandfather
la bisabuela – great grandmother
el tatarabuelo – great great grandfather
la tatarabuela – great great grandmother
el cuñado – brother-in-law
la cuñada – sister-in-law
el esposo – husband / spouse
la esposa – wife / spouse
el hermano – brother
la hermana – sister
el hermanastro – stepbrother
la hermanastra – stepsister
el medio hermano – half brother (*medio* is *adv.*)
la medio hermana – half sister (*medio* is *adverb*)
el hijo – son / child
la hija – daughter / child
el nieto – grandson / grandchild
la nieta – granddaughter / grandchild
el padre – father
el papá – dad
el papi – daddy
la madre – mother
la mamá – mom
la mami – mommy
el padrastro – stepfather / stepdad
la madrastra – stepmother / stepmom
el / la pariente/a – relative
el / la primo/a – cousin
el sobrino – nephew
la sobrina – niece
el suegro – father-in-law
la suegra – mother-in-law
el tío – uncle
la tía – aunt
el novio – boyfriend / groom
la novia – girlfriend / bride
el yerno – son-in-law
la nuera – daughter-in-law
el parentesco – family relationship / kinship
el / la gemelo/a – identical twin
el / la mellizo/a / cuate/a – fraternal twin
el / la antepasado/a / el ancestro – ancestor
estar casado/a (con) – to be married (to)
estar divorciado/a (de) – to be divorced
estar separado/a (de) – to be separated

estar soltero/a – to be single
estar muerto/a – to be dead
estar vivo/a – to be alive

las celebraciones
invitar – to invite
la invitación – invitation
la reunión (familiar) – meeting / family reunion
la tradición – tradition
la costumbre – custom
la celebración – celebration
celebrar – to celebrate
felicitar – to congratulate
¡Felicidades / Felicitaciones! – Congratulations!
la boda – wedding
casarse (con) – to get married (to)
el aniversario (de boda) – (wedding) anniversary
la fiesta de sorpresa – surprise party
la fiesta de cumpleaños – birthday party
el (los) cumpleaños (cumple) – birthday(s)
cumplir _____ años – to turn _____ years old
el nacimiento – birth
nacer (c → zc) – to be born
el funeral – funeral
morir(se) (o → ue) (o → u) – to die
el pastel – cake
la vela – candle
encender (e → ie) – to turn on / to light
apagar – to turn off / to extinguish
regalar – to give (as a gift)
dar – to give
charlar / platicar / hablar – to chat / to talk
cantar – to sing
bailar – to dance
el baile – dance
la graduación – graduation
graduarse – to graduate
el globo – balloon
el festival – festival
la feria – fair
explicar – to explain
decir (yo digo) (e → i) – to say / to tell
pedir (e → i) – to ask for / to request
servir (e → i) – to serve
el dulce – candy / sweet
empezar / comenzar (e → ie) – to start / to begin
terminar / acabar – to finish / to end
divertirse (e → ie) (e → i) – to have fun
aburrirse – to get bored
el / la aguafiestas – party pooper / wet blanket

pasarlo bien, mal – to have a good, bad time
decorar – to decorate
tomar / beber – to drink
comer – to eat
comprar – to buy
la flor – flower
la tarjeta (de cumpleaños) – (birthday) card
preguntar – to ask (a question)
tener lugar / ser – to take place
ir + a + *infinitivo* – to be going *to* _____

los días feriados
el día feriado / el día festivo – holiday
el día de boda, fiesta, etc. – wedding day, etc.
el Año Nuevo – New Year's Day
el Día de los Enamorados – Valentine's Day
el Día de la Madre – Mother's Day
el Día del Padre – Father's Day
el Día de la Independencia – Independence Day
los fuegos artificiales – fireworks
el Día de las Brujas – Halloween
el Día de (Acción de) Gracias – Thanksgiving
el pavo / el guajolote – turkey
el Hanukkah – Hanukkah
la Nochebuena – Christmas Eve
la Navidad – Christmas
la Nochevieja – New Year's Eve
el <u>2</u> de <u>abril</u> del <u>1984</u> – April 2, 1984

las bebidas alcohólicas (el alcohol)
el aguardiente – spirit (general)
la cerveza / la chela – beer
el champán / la champaña – champagne
la ginebra – gin
el jerez – sherry
el ron – rum
el tequila (*masculino*) – tequila
el vino (blanco, tinto) – (white, red) wine
el (la) vodka – vodka
la resaca / la cruda – hangover

para saludar y/o despedirse
abrazar – to hug
besar – to kiss
conocer (c → zc) – to know personally
            – to be familiar with
            – to meet
dar la mano – to shake hands
decir hola – to say hello
saludar – to greet
saludar con la mano – to wave
decir adiós – to say goodbye
despedirse (e → i) (de) – to say goodbye (to)

otras palabras y expresiones útiles
adorar – to adore
odiar – to hate
el odio – hate
amar – to love
el amor – love
reconocer (c → zc) – to recognize
el reconocimiento – recognition
encontrar (o → ue) / hallar – to find
buscar – to look for
gustar – to please / to be pleasing
el gusto – pleasure / (sense of) taste
faltar – to be missing / to be absent
quedar – to remain / to be remaining
llevar – to wear / to take / to carry
mientras – while
la gente – people
¿A qué edad …? – At what age …?
a los _____ años – at _____ years old
darse cuenta (de) – to realize
de nuevo / otra vez – again
especial – special
ver (yo veo) – to see / to watch
hecho/a a mano – made by hand
saber (yo sé) – to know (information, facts)
estar de acuerdo – to be in agreement
tener razón – to be right
el desastre – disaster
el éxito – success
¡No me digas! – You don't say. / No way!
el uno al otro – each other / one another

los pronombres de complemento reflexivo
me – myself   nos – ourselves
te – yourself   os – yourselves
se – himself / herself   se – themselves
    yourself   yourselves

los pronombres de complemento indirecto
me – me   nos – us
te – you   os – you
le – him / her / you   les – them / you

los pronombres de complemento directo
me – me   nos – us
te – you   os – you
lo / la – him / her / you   los / las – them / you
    it (thing)   them (things)

los adjetivos posesivos
mi(s) – my   nuestro/a(s) – our
tu(s) – your   vuestro/a(s) – your
su(s) – his / her / your   su(s) – their / your

Unidad 19 – de viaje

planear / planificar – to plan
viajar – to travel
el viaje – trip
la agencia de viajes – travel agency
el / la viajero/a – traveler
el país – country
ahorrar – to save (money or time)
gastar – to spend
vender – to sell
comprar – to buy
el boleto – ticket
    de ida y vuelta – roundtrip ticket
    sólo de ida – one-way ticket
el itinerario – itinerary
el horario – schedule
conseguir (e → i) – to get (physically) / to obtain
traer (allí → aquí) / llevar (aquí → allí) – to bring
la credencial / el carnet – form of identification
el pasaporte – passport
la guía turística – travel guide (book)
el lujo – luxury
la necesidad – necessity
el equipaje – luggage / baggage
la mochila – backpack
la maleta – suitcase
hacer la maleta / empacar – to pack
recomendar (e → ie) – to recommend
la recomendación – recommendation
reservar – to reserve
la reservación – reservation
la habitación simple – single room (one bed)
la habitación doble – double room (two beds)
sencillo/a / simple – simple
la ropa – clothing
los anteojos / las gafas / los lentes – glasses

el aeropuerto – airport
salir / partir – to leave / to depart
la salida – departure / exit
llegar – to arrive
la llegada – arrival
facturar (el equipaje) – to check (luggage)
recoger (el equipaje) – to pick up / to claim
la recogida de equipaje – baggage claim
pasar por – to go through / to pass by
el control de seguridad – security checkpoint
la aduana – customs
el / la aduanero/a – customs agent
mostrar (o → ue) – to show
el (la) terminal – terminal

el vuelo – flight
con destino a – with destination to / departing to
procedente de – originating in / arriving from
la escala – stop / layover
la demora – delay
esperar – to wait (for)
la aerolínea – airline

el avión – airplane
el / la pasajero/a – passenger
el / la piloto/a – pilot
el / la auxiliar de vuelo – flight attendant
despegar – to take off
aterrizar – to land
la salida de emergencia – emergency exit
el asiento – seat
sentarse (e → ie) – to sit (down)
el pasillo – aisle
la ventanilla – window (of a vehicle)
el cinturón de seguridad – seat belt / safety belt
abrocharse – to buckle (oneself) up
desabrocharse – to unbuckle (oneself)
la emergencia – emergency
el incendio – fire
en caso de – in case of
poner música – to put on music
los audífonos / los auriculares – headphones
el (la) radio – radio
encender (e → ie) / prender – to turn on
apagar – to turn off
el ventilador – fan
la luz, *pl.* las luces – light(s)
el / la turista – tourist

el dinero – money
la lana / la plata / la feria – money (slang: "dough")
el dinero en efectivo – cash
la moneda – coin / monetary unit
    cara o cruz (varies by country) – heads or tails
el billete – bill (money) / ticket
la cartera / el billetero – wallet / billfold
barato/a – cheap / inexpensive
caro/a / costoso/a – expensive
cambiar – to change / to exchange
la casa de cambio – currency-exchange place
la tasa de cambio – exchange rate
la tarjeta de crédito – credit card
la tarjeta de débito – debit card
el cheque de viajero – traveler's check
regatear – to haggle / to bargain

hacer una excursión – to go on an outing
la oficina de turismo – tourist office
el / la guía – guide (person)
la jornada – day's journey / day trip
el pueblo – town / indigenous peoples (as a group)
el / la indígena – indigenous (native) person
el mercado – market
la artesanía – handicraft / workmanship
el / la artesano/a – artisan
hecho/a a mano – made by hand
la joyería – jewelry / jewelry store
el recuerdo – souvenir / memory
incluir (y) – to include
disfrutar (de) – to enjoy
la naturaleza – nature
continuar (u → ú) – to continue
explorar – to explore
experimentar – to experience / to experiment
con toda confianza – with confidence (don't be shy)
tener confianza (en) – to be confident (in)
tener curiosidad (sobre) – to be curious (about)
tener cuidado (de / con) – to be careful (of / with)
tener miedo (a / de) – to be afraid (of)
suficiente / bastante – sufficient / enough
la llave – key
el llavero – keychain
el (reloj) despertador – alarm (clock)
regresar / volver (o → ue) – to return
el metro – subway
el autobús / el bus – bus (inter-city travel)
el camión – small bus (inner-city travel)
el (taxi) colectivo – minivan-style taxi
compartir (con) – to share (with)
colocar / poner – to put / to place / to set

la posesión
propio/a – own
el mío / la mía
   los míos / las mías – mine
el tuyo / la tuya
   los tuyos / las tuyas – yours
el suyo / la suya
   los suyos / las suyas – his / hers / yours
el nuestro / la nuestra
   los nuestros / las nuestras – ours
el vuestro / la vuestra
   los vuestros / las vuestras – yours (Spain)
el suyo / la suya
   los suyos / las suyas – theirs / yours (*pl.*)
cuyo/a – whose (gender based on possession)
   Ej. la persona cuyo carro …
      la persona cuya cartera …
      la persona cuyos amigos …
      la persona cuyas cosas …

el futuro / el porvenir – the future
antes de + *infinitivo* – before _____ing
después de + *infinitivo* – after _____ing
al + *infinitivo* – upon _____ing
ir a + *infinitivo* – to be going *to* _____
tener ganas de + *infinitivo* – to want *to* _____
querer + *infinitivo* – to want *to* _____
pensar + *infinitivo* – to plan *to* _____
preferir + *inf.* – to prefer *to* _____
tener que + *inf.* – to have *to* ___ (person specific)
hay que + *inf.* – to have *to* ____ / one must ____
necesitar + *infinitivo* – to need *to* _____
poder + *infinitivo* – to be able *to* _____
intentar + *infinitivo* – to try *to* _____
deber + *inf.* – to ought *to* (should / must) _____
a partir de (ayer, las 8:00) – as of (yesterday, 8:00)
de ahora en adelante – from now on

otras palabras y expresiones útiles
para + *infinitivo* – in order *to* _____
ya – already / now
apenas – barely / just now (time)
ni modo – oh well
ni siquiera – not even
¡(Mucho) ojo! – Pay (close) attention!
¡Aguas! – Watch out! / Look out!
¡Cuidado! – Careful!
¡Buen viaje! – Have a good trip!

los mandatos (el imperativo) (tú) – commands
gastar → gasta(lo) – spend (it)
   → no (lo) gastes – don't spend (it)
prender → prende(la) – turn (it) on
   → no (la) prendas – don't turn (it) on
compartir → comparte(melo) – share (it with me)
   → no (se lo) compartas – don't share (it
                  with him / her / them)

los mandatos irregulars (tú)
salir → sal – leave
   → no salgas – don't leave
traer → trae – bring
   → no traigas – don't bring
hacer → haz – do
   → no hagas – don't do
tener → ten – have
   → no tengas – don't have
poner → pon – put
   → no pongas – don't put
ir → ve – go
   → no vayas – don't go
ver → ve – look
   → no veas – don't look

Unidad 20 – las características

las cualidades – qualities (personality traits)

activo/a – active
alegre / feliz – happy
amigable – friendly
apasionado/a – passionate
capaz – capable
caprichoso/a – capricious / fickle
cariñoso/a – affectionate
celoso/a / envidioso/a – jealous / envious
compasivo/a – compassionate
complicado/a – complicated
comprensivo/a – understanding
confiable – trustworthy
considerado/a – considerate
coqueto/a – flirtatious
emocional – emotional
enojón / enojona – one who gets angry a lot
estúpido/a / tonto/a / bobo/a – stupid / dumb
exigente – demanding
franco/a – frank / straightforward
generoso/a – generous
gritón / gritona – one who yells a lot
hábil – skilled / skillful
humilde – humble / from a poor background
idealista – idealist / idealistic
imbécil / idiota – imbecile / idiot(ic)
impulsivo/a – impulsive
incomprensivo/a – not understanding
incapaz – incapable
ingenuo/a – naïve
íntimo/a – close / intimate
leal – loyal
mentiroso/a – liar
metiche / entremetido/a – nosey
modesto/a – modest
muy / bien – very
necio/a – foolish
optimista – optimist / optimistic
orgulloso/a – proud / prideful
perfeccionista – perfectionist
pesimista – pessimist / pessimistic
quejón / quejona – one who complains a lot
reservado/a – reserved
responsable – responsible
sensato/a – sensible
sensible – sensitive
sentimental – sentimental
sincero/a – sincere
talentoso/a – talented
tranquilo/a / quieto/a – calm / tranquil
vanidoso/a – vain

cómo nos relacionamos con otras personas

abusar (de) – to abuse
la actitud – attitude
admirar – to admire
el / la amigo/a / cuate/a – friend
la amistad – friendship / friend
apoyar – to support
burlarse (de) – to make fun (of)
el / la compañero/a – companion / mate
compartir (con) – to share (with)
comprometerse (con / a) – to commit (to)
el conflicto – conflict
caer (bien, mal) – (like *gustar*, but as a friend)
coquetear / flirtear – to flirt
confiar (i → í) (en) – to trust (in) / to confide (in)
el consejo – advice
dar consejo / aconsejar – to give advice
dejar de + *infinitivo* – to quit _____*ing*
los / las demás – the rest / the others
la discusión – discussion / argument
discutir – to discuss / to argue
enojarse / enfadarse (con) – to get angry (with)
entender (e → ie) / comprender – to understand
explicar – to explain
gozar (de) / disfrutar (de) – to enjoy
hacer caso (a) – to listen (to) / to mind / to obey
     No me hagas caso. – Never mind.
influir (y) (en / sobre) – to influence
intentar / tratar de + *infinitivo* – to try *to* _____
invitar – to invite
jurar – to swear (to promise)
llevarse (bien, mal) (con) – to get along (with)
el malentendido – misunderstanding
mantener (e → ie) – to maintain / to keep
obligar (a) – to compel / to obligate
el problema (*masculino*) / la bronca – problem
prometer – to promise
quejarse (de) – to complain (about)
rajarse – to back down / to back out
reírse (e → í) (e →) (de) – to laugh (at)
relacionarse (con) – to relate (with)
rendirse (e → i) / darse por vencido/a – to give up
resolver (o → ue) – to resolve / to solve
respetar – to respect
seguir (e → i) – to continue / to follow
seguir / continuar + -*ando*, -*iendo* – to keep ___*ing*
el sentido de humor – sense of humor
     tener un buen sentido … – to have a good …
surgir – to arise
tener en común (con) – to have in common (with)
visitar – to visit

los buenos modales – good manners

a sus (tus) órdenes – at your service
   a la orden – at your service
      para servir(le / te) – at your service
adelante – go ahead (of me)
agradecer (c → zc) – to thank
la bondad – kindness
   tener la bondad de + *inf.* – to be so kind as *to* ___
con permiso – excuse me (to pass by someone)
contar (o → ue) (con) – to count (on)
dar las gracias – to give thanks
   ¡Mil gracias! – Thank you so much!
de nada – you're welcome (it was nothing)
   por nada – it was nothing
   con mucho gusto – my pleasure
   (no hay) de qué – don't mention it
   no hay por qué – don't mention it
el gesto – (hand) gesture
perdón – excuse me (to ask for forgiveness)
   ¡Mil disculpas! – I'm so sorry! / Pardon me!
perdonar / disculpar – to pardon / to forgive
por favor – please
prestar – to lend / to loan
tomar prestado/a – to borrow

actividades en las que puedes participar

el asilo para ancianos – assisted-living home
el / la ayudante/a / asistente/a – helper / assistant
el club, *pl.* los clubs – club(s)
   el club rotario – rotary club
dar clases particulares – to give private lessons
el grupo – group
el individuo – individual (regardless of gender or sex)
individual – individual (*adjective*)
inscribirse / enrolarse (en) – to sign up / to enroll
el manicomio – insane asylum / mental hospital
el orfanatorio / el orfanato – orphanage
la redacción – writing
redactar – to write
tomar una clase – to take a class
trabajar como voluntario/a – to volunteer

los superlativos – superlatives

el / la más (+ *adjetivo*) – *the* most _____(-est) *one*
   lo más (+ *adjetivo*) – *the* most _____(-est) *thing*
el / la menos (+ *adjetivo*) – *the* least _____ *one*
   lo menos (+ *adjetivo*) – *the* least _____ *thing*
el / la mejor – *the* best *one*
   lo mejor – *the* best *thing*
el / la peor – *the* worst *one*
   lo peor – *the* worst *thing*
el que / *la* que – *the one* that
   lo que – what / *the thing* that

the many ways "to become"

convertirse (en) – often magical or fantastical
hacerse – often through effort
ponerse – often used with emotions
   Se puso triste. – She got (became) sad.
transformarse (en) – magical or through effort
llegar a ser – often used with professions
   Llegué a ser maestro. – I became a teacher.
volverse – often a mental transformation
   Se volvieron locos. – They went crazy.

otras palabras y expresiones útiles

abarcar – to encompass
además (de) – in addition (to) / besides
apropiado/a – appropriate
aunque – although / even though
averiguar – to check / to find out
la cantidad – quantity
a causa de + *sustantivo* – because of + *noun*
a causa de que + *verbo* – because + *verb*
acerca de / sobre – about
el / la ciudadano/a – citizen
consistir (en) / constar (de) – to consist (of)
contra – against
darse cuenta (de) – to realize
debido a – due to
decepcionar / defraudar / desilusionar – to disappoint
desperdiciar / malgastar – to waste
enterarse (de) – to find out (about)
la imagen – image
imaginar(se) – to imagine
inapropiado/a – inappropriate
el instinto – instinct
máximo/a – maximum
mínimo/a – minimum
   lo más mínimo – the slightest / bare minimum
mudarse – to move / to change residences
obtener / adquirir (i → ie) – to obtain / to acquire
personal – personal
sin embargo – nevertheless / however
tanto/a – so much
tanto/a como – as much as
tantos/as – so many
tantos/as como – as many as
valer (yo valgo) – to be worth
el valor – value / worth
valorar – to value
el talento – talent
la habilidad – ability
la destreza – skill (usually manual)
el don – (natural) gift
silbar / chiflar – to whistle
chasquear los dedos – to snap (one's fingers)

Unidad 21 – donde vivimos

la ciudad – the city
el apartamento / el departamento – apartment
el atasco – traffic jam
el / la ciclista – cyclist
la contaminación (del aire) – (air) pollution
la fuente – fountain / source
el peatón / la peatona – pedestrian
el (los) rascacielos – skyscraper(s)
las rejas – bars (on a window)
el tráfico – traffic
el transporte público – public transportation
urbano/a – urban (pertaining to the city)

el campo – the country
el aire libre – fresh air / open air
cultivar – to farm / to cultivate
el deber – duty / chore
el (los) espantapájaros – scarecrow(s)
la finca – country residence
el granero – barn
el / la granjero/a – farmer
la granja – farm
la naturaleza – nature
el paisaje – countryside / landscape
rural – rural (pertaining to the country)
el terreno – plot of land
el / la vaquero/a – cowboy / cowgirl

las zonas residenciales de las afueras – suburbs
el cerco / la cerca – fence
el farol – street light
el jardín – yard / garden
el tope / el policía acostado – speed bump
el transporte particular – private transportation
el / la vecino/a – neighbor
el vecindario / el barrio – neighborhood

las ventajas y desventajas de los tres
abundante – abundant / plentiful
afortunado/a – fortunate
    la fortuna – fortune
aislado/a – isolated
aislar (i → í) – to isolate
al alcance de la mano – within reach / accessible
alcanzar – to reach
aprovechar – to take advantage of (good)
    aprovecharse (de) algo, alguien – (selfishly)
amplio/a – ample / enough
animado/a – lively
animarse – to cheer up / to liven up

apurarse / apresurarse – to hurry / to rush
el asalto – assault
atar – to tie up / to tie down
bello/a / hermoso/a – beautiful
el beneficio – benefit
la calma – calm / calmness
caminar – to walk
comparar – to compare
la comunidad – community
contribuir (y) – to contribute
conveniente – suitable / convenient
convenir (e → ie) – to suit
el crimen – crime (serious, usually murder)
cruzar – to cross
decidir – to decide
dejar – to leave (behind)
dejar de + *infinitivo* – to quit _____ing
dejar / permitir – to let / to allow / to permit
la delincuencia – delincuency (generic crime)
el / la delincuente – delinquent / criminal
desatar – to unleash / to let loose
la desesperación – desperation / despair
desesperado/a – desperate
desesperar(se) – to despair / to panic
diario/a – daily (*adjective*)
a diario / diariamente – daily (*adverb*)
diferente / distinto/a – different / distinct
la diferencia – difference
la desventaja – disadvantage
la distancia (a) – distance (to)
la diversidad – diversity
desanimarse – to get discouraged
las drogas – drugs
escaparse – to escape
escuchar – to listen to
el espacio – space
estar en contacto (con) – to be in contact (with)
fenomenal – phenomenal
la gente – people
grave – serious / grave
el / la habitante – inhabitant
hay – there is / there are (*present*)
había – there was / there were (*imperfect*)
el homicidio – homicide
ideal – ideal
los impuestos – taxes
intentar + *inf.* / pretender + *inf.* -- to try *to* _____
loco/a – crazy
el ladrón / la ladrona – thief / burglar / robber
lamentar – to regret

la libertad (de) – (the) freedom (to)
leve – mild / slight
lindo/a – nice / cute / pretty
lleno/a (de gente) – full (of people)
maravilloso/a – marvelous / wonderful
matar – to kill
merecer(se) (c → zc) – to deserve
mudarse – to move / to change residences
ofrecer (c → zc) – to offer
oír (yo oigo) (y) – to hear
la oportunidad – opportunity
el (la) chance – chance / opportunity
parecer (c → zc) que – to seem that
el peligro – danger
peligroso/a – dangerous
pisar – to walk on / to tread on / to set foot on
la población – population
por un lado … – on (the) one hand …
por otro lado … – on the other hand …
puro/a – pure / sheer
el racismo – racism
racista – racist
rápido/a – fast / quick
robar – to steal / to rob
el robo – robbery
el ruido – noise
sano/a – healthy
seguro/a – safe
semejante / similar / parecido/a – similar
la semejanza – similarity
severo/a – severe
sin embargo / no obstante – nevertheless
situado/a – situated
la sociedad – society
sublime – sublime
la suerte – luck
suertudo/a – lucky
tardar (en) – to take (time) (to)
la tranquilidad – tranquility / calmness
tranquilizar / calmar – to calm
tratar bien, mal – to treat well, badly
la ubicación – location
ubicar / localizar – to locate
ubicarse (estar ubicado/a) – to be located
la ventaja – advantage
vale la pena – it's worth it / it's worth the trouble
vivir – to live
la vida – life
    social – social life
      nocturna – night life
la violencia – violence
visitar – to visit
las viviendas / el alojamiento – housing

por donde andamos
la acera / la banqueta – sidewalk
el atajo – shortcut
la autopista / la carretera – highway
la avenida – avenue
la calle – street
el camino – path / walkway
el cruce – crosswalk / intersection
la encrucijada / la intersección – intersection
el peaje – toll
el puente – bridge
la ruta – route
el sendero / la vereda – trail / path
dar una vuelta – to go around / to take a walk
dar media vuelta – to turn around
dar marcha atrás – to back up / to reverse
manejar / conducir (c → zc) – to drive
andar / pasear – to go (around, about) / to walk

las señales de tránsito – traffic signals
ALTO / PARE / STOP – STOP
CEDA EL PASO – YIELD
SENTIDO ÚNICO – ONE WAY
NO ESTACIONAR – NO PARKING
VELOCIDAD MÁXIMA – SPEED LIMIT
NO ADELANTAR – NO PASSING
el semáforo – traffic light
incorporarse (a) – to merge (with)

otras palabras y expresiones útiles
el origen – origin
todavía / aún – still / yet
ya – already / now
así – like this / like that (in this/that way)
así que … – (and) so …
fuera – out
fuera de – outside of / out of / beyond
    fuera de control – out of control
    fuera de servicio – out of order (not working)
afuera – outside
dentro – in
dentro de – within
adentro – inside
cualquier – any (before *singular noun*)
    cualquier cosa – anything
cualesquier – any (before *plural noun*)
cualquiera – any one
cualesquiera – any ones
¿Y qué? – So what?
de todos los tiempos – of all time
en absoluto – at all (in a negative sentence)
con respecto a / respecto de – with respect to
en relación con / con relación a – in relation to

Unidad 22 – el entretenimiento

cómo vemos la televisión y las películas
alquilar / rentar – to rent
la audiencia – audience
la antena – antenna
cambiar – to change
el canal – channel
devolver (o → ue) – to return (an item)
el dividí / el DVD – DVD
filmar – to film
grabar – to record
el público – (the) public / (the) audience
la televisión por cable – cable TV
la televisión por satélite – satellite TV
ver – to see / to watch
mirar – to watch / to look at

la televisión, las películas y su influencia
absurdo/a – absurd
aburrido/a – boring (ser)
        – bored (estar)
acerca de / sobre – about
el actor – actor
la actriz, *pl.* las actrices – actress(es)
afectar – to affect
analizar – to analyze
anunciar – to announce
el anuncio – announcement
argüir (y) – to debate / to argue
el argumento – argument / stance on a subject
ayudar (a) – to help (to)
bostezar – to yawn
la calidad – quality
    de alta calidad – high quality
    de baja calidad – low quality
chillar – to scream
chistoso/a / gracioso/a – funny
el cine (cinema) – cinema / movie theater
comprobar (o → ue) – to prove
el comentario – commentary / comment
comentar – to comment
el comercial – commercial
conmover (o → ue) – to move (emotionally)
conmovedor/a – (emotionally) moving
controlar – to control
criticar – to critique / to criticize
crítico/a – critic / critical
la crítica – critique / criticism
dañoso/a / dañino/a – harmful
dar – to give
de acción – action
de ciencia ficción – science fiction

de comedia – comedy
de fantasía – fantasy
deportivo/a – sports
de terror – horror / scary
demasiado/a – too much
el derecho (a) – (the) right (to)
la discusión – discussion / argument
la desnudez – nudity
desnudo/a / encuerado/a – nude / naked
los dibujos animados – cartoons
doblado/a – dubbed (into another language)
el documental – documentary
el drama (*masculino*) – drama
el efecto – effect
emocionarse – to get excited
emocionado/a – excited
emocionante – exciting
enfocarse (en) – to focus (on)
enseñar – to teach / to show
entretener(se) (e → ie) – to entertain (oneself)
entretenido/a – entertaining (ser)
        – entertained (estar)
el entretenimiento – entertainment
la entrevista – interview
entrevistar – to interview
el episodio – episode
equivocarse – to be wrong / to make a mistake
la escena – scene
el estilo – style
evaluar (u → ú) – to evaluate
exagerado/a – exaggerated
exagerar – to exaggerate
extranjero/a – foreign
extraño/a / raro/a – weird
fascinante – fascinating
fascinar – to fascinate
fijarse (en) – to take notice (of) / to fixate (on)
la furia – fury
hacer / causar / ocasionar – to make / to cause
hacer daño / causar daño / ocasionar daño – to harm
importar – to matter / to be important
la imagen – image
la influencia – influence
influenciar / influir (y) (en / sobre) – to influence
el infomercial – infomercial
la información – information
informativo/a – informative
inmediato/a – immediate
inmediatamente / de inmediato – immediately
interpretar – to interpret
interesante – interesting

interesar – to interest
la ira – wrath / rage
llorar – to cry
el / la locutor/a – speaker
manipular – to manipulate
mediocre – mediocre
el miedo – fear
negativo/a – negative
notar – to note / to take note of
las noticias – (the) news
opinar – to be of an opinion / to have an opinion
la opinión – opinion
la película (peli) / el filme – movie / film
el pensamiento – thought
pensar (e → ie) – to think
la percepción – perception
el personaje – character (in a movie, show, etc.)
la pesadilla – nightmare
policiaco/a / policíaco/a – police / detective
por eso – for that / that's why / therefore
positivo/a – positive
preocuparse (de) – to worry (oneself) (about)
prestar/poner atención (a) – to pay attention (to)
profundo/a / hondo/a – profound / deep
    poco profundo/a – shallow
el programa (*masculino*) – show / program
prohibir (i → í) – to prohibit
el pronóstico de tiempo – weather forecast
el pudor – modesty (often sexual or body shame)
el punto de vista – point of view
reír(se) (e → í) (e →) (de) – to laugh (at)
el reportaje – (news) report
reportar – to report
el / la reportero/a – reporter
representar – to represent
ridículo/a – ridiculous
la risa – laughter
la rabia – rage / anger
el romance – romance
romántico/a – romantic
el secreto – secret
la secuela – sequel
según – according to
la serie – series
el significado – meaning
sin supervisión – without supervision
la sociedad – society
soñar (o → ue) (con) – to dream (about)
    el sueño – dream
los subtítulos – subtitles
tal como, *pl.* tales como – such as
la telenovela – soap opera
la temporada – season (of a TV series)

tener razón – to be right
el tipo / la clase – type / class
el tráiler / el corto / el avance – trailer
tras – after
    uno/a tras otro/a – one after the other
tratarse (de) – to be about
la vergüenza – embarrassment / shame / disgrace
vergonzoso/a – embarrassing / shameful / disgraceful
violento/a – violent

para hablar de la hora
a las 19:30 horas – at 19:30 hours
a eso de las 20:00 horas – at about 8:00 PM
desde – from
durar – to last
en estreno – debut / premier / for the first time
estrenarse / salir – to debut / to come out
en punto – on the dot
hasta – until
recientemente – recently
es la 1:00 pasada – it's past 1:00
son las 3:00 pasadas – it's past 3:00
pasada la 1:00 – after 1:00
pasadas las 10:00 – after 10:00

la censura – censor / censorship
censurar – to censor
la clasificación – rating / classification
clasificar – to rate / to classify
apto/a para toda la familia – suitable for the
                            whole family
prohibido/a para menores – minors prohibited
se recomienda discreción – viewer discretion
                            advised
estar a favor (de) – to be in favor (of)
estar en contra (de) – to be against
apaciguar / pacificar – to appease / to pacify

otros medios de comunicación
a través de / por medio de – through / by way of
el (la) internet / la red – (the) internet
el periódico / el diario – newspaper
el (la) radio – radio
la revista – magazine

el imperfecto progresivo
estar + *gerundio* (-*ing* form) – to be _____*ing*
    ¿Qué estabas haciendo? – What were you doing?
    Estaba levantando pesas. – I was lifting weights.
cuando – when
mientras – while (at the same time)
mientras que – whereas (used for contrast)

Unidad 23 – el medioambiente y la naturaleza

el medioambiente – (the) environment
el (la) mar / el océano – sea / ocean
la ola – wave
la orilla – shore / shoreline
la costa – coast
la marea – tide
la corriente – current
la deriva – drift
a la deriva – adrift
el delfín, *pl.* los delfines – dolphin(s)
el pulpo – octopus
el calamar – squid
la almeja – clam
el mejillón, *pl.* los mejillones – mussel(s)
la ostra – oyster
la concha – shell
la ballena – whale
la ballena asesina / la orca – killer whale
el cachalote – sperm whale
el león marino, *pl.* los leones marinos – sea lion(s)
la morsa – walrus
la foca – seal
el tiburón, *pl.* los tiburones – shark(s)
la langosta – lobster
el cangrejo – crab
el arrecife – reef
el coral – coral
las algas – algae / seaweed
el río – river
el cauce – riverbed
el (la) margen, *pl.* los márgenes – river bank(s)
la trucha – trout
el salmón, *pl.* los salmones – salmon
el riachuelo – brook / stream
el arroyo – creek
el lago – lake
la charca – pond
el pantano – swamp / marsh
el cocodrilo – crocodile
el caimán, *pl.* los caimanes – alligator(s)
el lagarto – lizard
la lagartija – small lizard
la serpiente / la culebra – snake
el reptil – reptile
el anfibio – amphibian
la rana – frog
el renacuajo – tadpole
el sapo – toad
el árbol – tree
la rama – branch

la corteza (de árbol) – (tree) bark
el bosque – forest
la selva tropical – tropical rainforest
frondoso/a – thick with leaves, branches, trees
la planta – plant
la hoja – leaf
el tallo – stem / stalk
el pétalo – petal
la raíz, *pl.* las raíces – root(s)
fructuoso/a – fruitful / successful
infructuoso/a – fruitless / unsuccessful
dar fruto(s) – to bear fruit / to be successful
fértil – fertile
estéril – barren
la semilla – seed
sembrar (e → ie) – to sow / to plant seeds / to seed
la siembra – planting / sowing
cosechar – to harvest / to reap
la cosecha – harvest
el (los) oasis – oasis (oases)
el espejismo – mirage
la isla – island
el paraíso – paradise
el archipiélago – archipelago
el / la depredador/a – predator
la presa – prey
el mamífero – mammal
el puerco espín – porcupine
el castor – beaver
el mapache – raccoon
el zorrillo / la mofeta – skunk
el glotón, *pl.* los glotones – wolverine(s)
el tejón, *pl.* los tejones – badger(s)
feroz – ferocious
la ardilla – squirrel
el zorro – fox
el lobo – wolf
el coyote – coyote
la nutria – otter
el elefante – elephant
la jirafa – giraffe
el rinoceronte – rhinoceros
el hipopótamo – hippopotamus
el puma (*masculino*) – mountain lion / cougar
el tigre – tiger
el león, *pl.* los leones – lion(s)
el jaguar – jaguar
el leopardo – leopard
el guepardo – cheetah
la pantera – panther

la hiena – hyena
el avestruz, *pl.* los avestruces – ostrich(es)
veloz – fast / quick / fleet / speedy
el canguro – kangaroo
el ornitorrinco – (duckbilled) platypus
el bisonte – bison
el alce – elk / moose
el venado / el ciervo – deer
el oso (pardo, polar) – (brown, polar) bear
el cerdo / el cochino / el guarro – pig
la bestia de carga – beast of burden
el buey – ox
el ave (*femenino*) / el pájaro – bird
la rapaz, *pl.* las rapaces – raptor(s)
el búho / la lechuza – owl
el águila (*femenino*), *pl.* las águilas – eagle(s)
el halcón, *pl.* los halcones – hawk(s) / falcon(s)
el cóndor, *pl.* los cóndores – condor(s)
el (los) albatros – albatross(es)
la gaviota – seagull
el pingüino – penguin
el pelícano – pelican
el tucán, *pl.* los tucanes – toucan(s)
la cigüeña – stork
el colibrí, *pl.* los colibríes – hummingbird(s)
el pájaro carpintero – woodpecker
el ganso – goose
el pato – duck
el insecto – insect
el escarabajo – beetle
la hormiga – ant
el (los) ciempiés – centipede(s)
el (los) milpiés – millipede(s)
la mariposa – butterfly
la libélula – dragonfly
la luciérnaga – firefly / lightning bug
el arácnido – arachnid
la araña – spider
el alacrán / el escorpión – scorpion
la manada – small pack (wolves), herd, flock, etc.
el ganado – livestock (cattle, bison, etc.)
la bandada – flock (birds), school (fish), etc.
el rebaño – large flock (sheep), etc.
terrestre – terrestrial (pertaining to land)
marítimo/a – maritime (pertaining to the sea)
las placas tectónicas – tectonic plates
la atmósfera / la atmosfera – atmosphere
la capa de ozono – ozone layer
el iceberg, *pl.* los icebergs – iceberg(s)
el glaciar – glacier
amarillento/a / amarilloso/a – yellowish
azulado/a / azuloso/a – bluish
verdoso/a – greenish

verde azulado – bluish green
incoloro/a – colorless
el olor (a) – smell (of)
inodoro/a – odorless
apestar – to stink
el metano – methane
el oxígeno – oxygen
el hidrógeno – hydrogen
el nitrógeno – nitrogen
el dióxido de carbono – carbon dioxide
advertir (e → ie) (e → i) – to warn
la advertencia – warning
atreverse a + *infinitivo* – to dare *to* _____
los animales salvajes – wild animals
las plantas silvestres – wild plants
el cacto / el (los) cactus – cactus (cacti / cactuses)
psicodélico/a – psychedelic
el hongo – mushroom
el peyote – peyote
venenoso/a – poisonous / venemous
envenenar – to poison
el fuego – fire
la fogata – campfire
la leña – firewood / lumber
el palo – stick
ligero/a – light-weight
pesado/a – heavy
mojado/a – wet
seco/a – dry
contaminado/a – polluted / contaminated
romper – to break / to tear
esperar – to hope (for)
suplicar / rogar (o → ue) – to plead / to beg
conservar – to conserve
prometer – to promise
la promesa – promise
olvidar – to forget
perder (e → ie) – to lose
perdido/a – lost
el amanecer / el alba (*femenino*) – dawn
el anochecer – nightfall
la puesta del sol / el atardecer – sunset
las tinieblas / la oscuridad – darkness
la luz, *pl.* las luces – light(s)
el crepúsculo – twilight
el silencio – silence
el sonido – noise
el parque nacional – national park
la colina – hill
el valle – valley
la montaña – mountain
el prado / la pradera / la llanura / la vega
    – (the) plains / meadow / prairie / lowlands

la sombra – shadow / shade
peligroso/a – dangerous
en peligro de extinción – endangered
extinto/a – extinct
en cautiverio – captive / in captivity
hundir – to sink
proteger – to protect
escoger – to choose
el hoyo / el agujero / el hueco – hole
la grieta – crack
la cueva / la caverna – cave / cavern
el murciélago – bat
reciclar – to recycle
el reciclaje / el reciclamiento – recycling
reciclable – recyclable
la meta – goal
establecer (c → zc) – to establish / to set
lograr – to achieve / to accomplish
lograr + *infinitivo* / conseguir (e → i) + *infinitivo*
    – to manage *to* _____ / to succeed at _____*ing*
tener sentido – to make sense
callar – to (make) quiet (down)
al azar – randomly / at random
el líder / la lideresa – leader
el liderazgo – leadership
echar un vistazo (a) – to take a look (at)
tomar medidas – to take measures
descartar – to discard / to throw out
desechable – disposable
despreciar – to disregard / to discount / to despise
menospreciar – to undervalue / to think nothing of
apreciar – to appreciate / to think highly of
hurgar – to rummage
el recordatorio – reminder
acudir (a) – to show up (to)
obstinado/a / terco/a – obstinate / stubborn
la avaricia / la codicia – greed
avaricioso/a / codicioso/a – greedy
egoísta – selfish
privilegiado/a – privileged
priorizar – to prioritize
la excusa / el pretexto – excuse
feo/a – ugly
bello/a / hermoso/a – beautiful
embellecer (c → zc) – to make beautiful
florecer (c → zc) – to flourish / to bloom
entristecer (c → zc) / agüitar – to sadden
agobiar / abrumar – to overwhelm
cansar / agotar – to exhaust
desgastarse / deteriorarse – to wear/waste away
el volcán, *pl.* los volcanes – volcano(s)
erupcionar – to erupt
la ceniza – ash

tumbar – to knock over / to knock down
derribar / demoler (o → ue) – to demolish
arruinar – to ruin
arrasar / destruir (y) – to raze / to destroy
talar – to cut down
el desastre (natural) – (natural) disaster
el tornado – tornado
el huracán, *pl.* los huracanes – hurricane(s)
la inundación – flood
inundar – to flood
la avalancha – avalanche
el deslave – mudslide / landslide
escaso/a – scarce
la escasez – scarcity / shortage
la sequía – drought
el recurso (natural) – (natural) resource
el oro (dorado/a) – gold (golden)
la plata (plateado/a) – silver
el cobre – copper
el mineral – mineral
el gas natural – natural gas
el petróleo – oil / petroleum
el calentamiento global – global warming
el cambio climático – climate change
el clima (*masculino*) – climate / weather
la meteorología – meteorology
la consecuencia – consequence
las repercusiones – repercussions
la superficie – surface
la certidumbre – certainty
la incertidumbre – uncertainty
la muchedumbre – masses (of people, etc.)
el / la hipócrita – hypocrite
la hipocresía – hypocrisy
pasmado/a / boquiabierto/a – aghast / stunned
intimidar – to intimidate
intimidante – intimidating
bajo – under / underneath
a la intemperie / al aire libre – out in the open
los detalles / los pormenores – details

otras expresiones útiles
estar a punto de + *infinitivo* – to be about *to* _____
tener en mente / en cuenta – to keep in mind
tomar en cuenta – to take into account
haber de / tener que – to have *to* _____
    Ej. He de hacerlo. / Tengo que hacerlo.
ser tiempo de + *infinitivo* – to be time *to* _____
    Ej. Es tiempo de buscar otro trabajo.
ser hora de + *infinitivo* – to be time (of day) *to* ___
    Ej. Era hora de cenar.
cada vez más – more and more
una y otra vez – over and over (again)

Unidad 24 – los misterios, los fenómenos y los complots

la religión y las creencias – religion and beliefs
afirmar – to affirm
el alma (*femenino*), *pl*. las almas – soul(s)
el altar – altar
ateo/a – atheist
el chamán / la chamana – shaman
cierto/a / verdadero/a – certain / true
comprobar (o → ue) – to prove
confesar (e → ie) – to confess
la conjetura – conjecture
convencer (c → z) – to convince
creer (en, que) – to believe (in, that)
el culto – cult
el / la curandero/a – healer
el desierto – (the) desert
el dios – god
la diosa – goddess
la duda – doubt
dudar – to doubt
enterrar (e → ie) / sepultar – to bury
la especulación – speculation
especular – to speculate
el espíritu – spirit
falso/a – false
la fe – faith
el homenaje – homage
   rendir (e → i) homenaje – to pay homage
imposible – impossible
investigar – to investigate
negar (e → ie) – to deny
negarse a + *infinitivo* – to refuse *to* _____
la ofrenda – offering
posible – possible
la prueba – test
rezar / orar – to pray
el ritual – ritual
sacrificar – to sacrifice
el sacrificio – sacrifice
la secta – sect
la señal – sign / signal
la sepultura – grave
suponer – to suppose
supuesto/a / dizque – supposed / so-called
el tabú, *pl*. los tabúes – taboo(s)
el / la testigo – witness
la tribu – tribe
el tributo – tribute
   pagar tributo – to pay tribute
la tumba / el sepulcro – tomb
el vudú – voodoo

la mitología y la cultura – mythology and culture
acordarse (o → ue) (de) – to remember
aparecer (c → zc) – to appear
la aparición – apparition
construir (y) – to build / to construct
cultural – cultural
desaparecer (c → zc) – to disappear
desconocido/a – unknown
el / la duende/a – goblin / elf
encantado/a – enchanted
enorme – enormous
los escalofríos – (the) chills
la escultura – sculpture
la estatua – statue
la estructura – structure
la evidencia – evidence
existir – to exist
explicable – explainable
extraño/a – weird / strange
extraordinario/a – extraordinary
el fantasma (*masculino*) – ghost
el fenómeno – phenomenon
la figura – figure / shape
el / la gigante/a – giant
gigantesco/a – gigantic
el / la gnomo/a – dwarf / troll / gnome
el hada (*femenino*) – fairy (regardless of gender or sex)
la huella – print / track
inexplicable – unexplainable / inexplicable
legendario/a – legendary
la leyenda – legend
el lugar / el sitio – place / site
el misterio – mystery
misterioso/a – mysterious
el mito – myth
mitológico/a – mythological
el monstruo – monster (regardless of gender or sex)
mover (o → ue) – to move
el / la ogro/a – ogre
el peregrinaje – pilgrimage
el / la peregrino/a – pilgrim / traveler
pertenecer (c → zc) (a) – to pertain / to belong (to)
la piedra – rock / stone
la piel de gallina – goosebumps
la pirámide – pyramid
el rastro – trace
el reporte / la noticia – report / piece of news
rodear – to surround / to circle
la rueda – wheel
la sensación – sensation / feeling

sobrenatural – supernatural
la teoría – theory
teórico/a – theoretical
la travesía – journey / voyage
el Triángulo de las Bermudas – the Bermuda Triangle

las medidas – measurements / measures
calcular – to calculate / to figure
medir (e → i) – to measure
el metro – meter
el centímetro – centimeter
el milímetro – millimeter
el pie – foot (12 inches)
la pulgada – inch
la yarda – yard (3 feet)
estrecho/a / angosto/a – narrow
así de estrecho/a – like this narrow (w/hand gesture)
ancho/a – wide
(así) de ancho/a – (like this wide) in width
la anchura – width
alto/a – tall / high
(así) de alto/a – (like this tall) in height
la altura – height
grande – big / large
la grandeza – greatness / grandeur
así de grande – like this big
pequeño/a / chico/a – small
así de pequeño/a – like this small
largo/a – long
la largura / la longitud – length
(así) de largo/a – (like this long) in length
como – like / as
el diámetro – diameter
pesar – to weigh
la tonelada – ton
la libra – pound
el kilogramo – kilogram

el horóscopo – horoscope
el signo del Zodiaco – Zodiac sign
Aries – Aries
Tauro – Taurus
Géminis – Gemini
Cáncer – Cancer
Leo – Leo
Virgo – Virgo
Libra – Libra
Escorpio – Scorpio
Sagitario – Sagittarius
Capricornio – Capricorn
Acuario – Aquarius
Piscis – Pisces
predecir (e → i) – to predict

el universo – (the) universe
la galaxia – galaxy
la Vía Láctea – (The) Milky Way
el sistema solar (*masculino*) – solar system
el sol – (the) sun
el planeta (*masculino*) – planet
　　Mercurio – Mercury
　　Venus – Venus
　　Tierra – Earth
　　Marte – Mars
　　Júpiter – Jupiter
　　Saturno – Saturn
　　Urano – Uranus
　　Neptuno – Neptune
　　Plutón – Pluto
la luna (llena, nueva) – (full, new) moon
la estrella – star
la estrella fugaz – shooting star
el cometa (*masculino*) – comet
el asteroide – asteroid
el meteorito – meteorite
el eclipse (lunar, solar) – (lunar, solar) eclipse
el rayo – ray
la aurora boreal – aurora borealis (northern lights)
la aurora austral – aurora australis (southern lights)
el solsticio – solstice
el equinoccio – equinox
emitir – to emit
iluminar / alumbrar – to illuminate / to light
brillar / resplandecer (c → zc) – to shine / to glow
terrestre – terrestrial / of Earth
extraterrestre – extraterrestrial / alien
el / la marciano/a – Martian
el ovni (objeto volador no identificado) – UFO
la nave espacial – spaceship
volar (o → ue) – to fly
el / la astronauta – astronaut
vaciar (i → í) – to empty
vacío/a – empty

otras palabras y expresiones útiles
a pesar de (que) – in spite of (the fact that)
aunque – although / even though
el complot – plot / conspiracy
conspirar – to conspire / to plot
de la nada – out of nowhere
de repente – suddenly / all of a sudden
en medio de la nada – in the middle of nowhere
entonces / pues – so / well / then / therefore
estar convencido/a (de) – to be convinced (of)
estar seguro/a (de) – to be sure (of)
que yo sepa – that I know of / as far as I know
todo con medida – everything in moderation

Unidad 25 – el cuerpo humano y la medicina

la anatomía – anatomy
el abdomen – abdomen
las amígdalas – tonsils
el apéndice (vermicular) – appendix
el antebrazo – forearm
la arteria – artery
la articulación, *pl.* las articulaciones – joint(s)
la axila / el sobaco – underarm / armpit
la barbilla – chin
el bazo – spleen
la boca – mouth
    bucal – mouth (*adjective*)
el brazo – arm
la cabeza – head
la cadera – hip
la cara / el rostro – face
el cartílago – cartilage
la ceja – eyebrow
la célula – cell
el cerebro / el seso – brain
    los sesos – brains
el cérvix / el cuello uterino – cervix
la cintura – waist
el codo – elbow
el colon – colon
la columna vertebral / espina dorsal – spinal column
el corazón – heart
la costilla – rib
el cuello – neck
el cuerpo – body
    corporal – body (*adjective*)
el dedo – finger
    el meñique – pinky
    el dedo anular – ring finger
    el dedo mayor / el dedo corazón – middle finger
    el dedo índice – index finger
    el pulgar – thumb
el dedo de pie – toe
    el dedo gordo – big toe
el diente / la muela – tooth / molar
las encías – gums
la entrepierna – inner thigh
el (la) enzima – enzyme
el esmalte – enamel
el esófago – esophagus
la espalda – back
el esqueleto – skeleton
el estómago – stomach
    estomacal – stomach (*adjective*)
    los jugos gástricos – gastric juices
la frente – forehead

las fosas nasales – nostrils
el ganglio/nódulo linfático – lymph node
la garganta – throat
los genitales – genitals
la glándula (suprarrenal) – (adrenal) gland
el glóbulo (blanco, rojo) – (white, red) blood cell
el hígado – liver
el hombro – shoulder
el hueso – bone
la ingle – groin
el intestino / la tripa – intestine
    las tripas – guts
el labio – lip
la lengua – tongue
el ligamento – ligament
la mandíbula – jaw
la mano (*femenino*) – hand
la médula – (bone) marrow
la mejilla / el cachete – cheek
la muñeca – wrist
el músculo – muscle
el muslo – thigh
las nalgas – buttocks
la nariz, *pl.* las narices – nose(s)
el nervio – nerve
el nudillo – knuckle
el oído – inner ear
el ojo – eye
el ombligo – navel / belly button
la oreja – outer ear
el órgano – organ
la palma – palm
el páncreas – pancreas
la panza / la barriga / el vientre – belly
la pantorrilla (los gemelos) – calf (calf muscles)
el párpado – eyelid
el pecho – chest
el pelo / el cabello – hair
el pene – penis
la pestaña – eyelash
    pestañear / parpadear – to blink
el pezón, *pl.* los pezones – nipple(s)
el pie – foot
la piel – skin
la pierna – leg
el pubis – pubic region
el pulmón, *pl.* los pulmones – lung(s)
la retina – retina
el riñón, *pl.* los riñones – kidney(s)
la rodilla – knee
la sangre – blood

el seno / la mama – breast
el talón, *pl.* los talones – heel(s)
el tejido – tissue
el tendón, *pl.* los tendones – tendon(s)
el testículo – testicle
el tobillo – ankle
el torso – torso
la uña – fingernail / toenail
el útero / la matriz – uterus / womb
la vagina – vagina
el vaso sanguíneo – blood vessel
la vejiga – bladder
la vena – vein
la vesícula biliar – gall bladder
la vulva – vulva

las descripciones
alto/a – tall
la altura / la estatura – height / stature
    de estatura mediana – medium height
    de gran altura – of great stature (tall)
bajo/a / chaparro/a – short
de piel blanca (blanco/a) – white
de piel negra (negro/a) – black
de piel oscura / morena (moreno/a) – dark-skinned
de tercera edad – senior
    edad avanzada – advanced age
delgado/a – thin
demacrado/a / emaciado/a – emaciated
demacrarse – to waste away
estar de/en buena forma – to be in good shape
flaco/a – skinny
gordo/a – fat
obeso/a – obese
indigente – indigent
diestro/a – righthanded
zurdo/a – lefthanded
rubio/a – blonde
pelirrojo/a – redhead
moreno/a – brunette
de pelo castaño/moreno – brown-haired
de pelo canoso – gray-haired
las canas – gray hairs
menor de edad – minor (underage)
sano/a – healthy / in good health
medir (e → ie) (e → i) – to measure
    ¿Cuánto mide el paciente?
    El paciente mide 175 centímetros.
la libra – pound (lb.)
subir de peso / ganar peso – to gain weight
    subir de peso 5 libras / ganar 5 libras
bajar de peso / perder peso – to lose weight
    bajar de peso 10 libras / perder 10 libras

pesar – to weigh
    La paciente pesa 145 libras.
    La asistenta médica pesó al paciente.
¿Qué tan + *adjetivo*? – How _____?
¿Qué tan obeso es? – How obese is he?
¿Cuán + *adjetivo*? – How _____?
¿Cuán delgado es? – How thin is he?
tener sobrepeso – to be overweight
la orientación sexual – sexual orientation
    bisexual – bisexual
    gay (pronounced "*guey*") – gay
    heterosexual – heterosexual
    homosexual – homosexual
    lesbiano/a / lésbico/a – lesbian
    transexual – transgender

los problemas y las enfermedades
el aborto espontáneo – miscarriage
el abuso – abuse (usually sexual)
la adicción / las adicciones – addiction(s)
    ser adicto/a (a) – to be addicted (to)
las agruras / la acidez estomacal – heartburn
el alcohol – alcohol
el / la alcohólico/a – alcoholic
el alcoholismo – alcoholism
la alergia – allergy
    ser alérgico/a (a) – to be allergic (to)
los altibajos – highs and lows / ups and downs
    los bajos – lows (mood, energy, etc.)
    los altos – highs (mood, energy, etc.)
la amigdalitis – tonsillitis
la ampolla – blister
la ansiedad – anxiety
la apendicitis – appendicitis
la arruga – wrinkle
la artritis (reumatoide) – (rheumatoid) arthritis
el asma (*femenino*) – asthma
el autismo – autism
la bacteria / el germen – bacteria / germ
bacteriano/a – bacterial
balbucear / tartamudear – to stutter / to stammer
benigno/a – benign
caerse (yo me caigo) – to fall accidentally
la caída – fall
el calambre – cramp
el callo – callus
el cáncer (metastásico) – (metastatic) cancer
canceroso/a – cancerous
el cancerígeno / el carcinógeno – carcinogen
cardiaco/a / cardíaco/a – cardiac
la(s) caries dentaria(s) – dental cavity (cavities)
la ceguera – blindness
ciego/a – blind

la cicatriz, *pl.* las cicatrices – scar(s)
la cirrosis – cirrhosis
el coágulo / el cuajarón sanguíneo – blood clot
el colesterol alto/elevado – high cholesterol
colorrectal – colorectal
el coma (*masculino*) – coma
    caer en coma – to fall into a coma
las complicaciones – complications
concebir (e → i) – to conceive
la concepción – conception
la conjuntivitis – conjunctivitis
la conmoción cerebral – concussion
(estar) constipado/a – to have a stuffy nose
contagiarse (de) / contraer – to contract
contagioso/a – contagious
las contracciones – contractions
la crisis – attack / fit
    alérgica – allergy attack
    asmática – asthma attack
    cerebral / convulsiva – seizure
    epiléptica – epileptic fit / seizure
dar positivo por ____ – to test positive for ____
la demencia – dementia
la depresión – depression
deprimente – depressing
deprimido/a – depressed
deprimir – to depress
el derrame cerebral / el infarto cerebral – stroke
desangrar – to bleed out
el desencadenante – trigger
la deshidratación – dehydration
deshidratado/a – dehydrated
desmayarse – to pass out / to faint
la diabetes – diabetes
la(s) diagnosis – diagnosis (diagnoses)
la diarrea – diarrhea
el dolor (agudo) – (sharp) pain
la drogadicción – drug addiction
    ser drogadicto/a – to be a drug addict
drogado/a – drugged
ebrio/a / borracho/a / tomado/a – intoxicated / drunk
el efecto secundario – side effect
embarazada – pregnant
el embarazo – pregnancy
    ectópico – ectopic pregnancy
embarazarse (de) – to get pregnant (with)
enfermarse – to get sick
la enfermedad / la afección – illness / disease
la enfermedad transmitida sexualmente – STD
el entumecimiento – numbness
entumecido/a – numb
entumirse – to fall asleep (body part)
envenenarse – to be poisoned

la espinilla / el grano – pimple / zit
la esquizofrenia – schizophrenia
el estornudo – sneeze
estornudar – to sneeze
estreñido/a – constipated
el estreñimiento – constipation
estreñirse (e → i) – to become constipated
el factor – factor
la flema – phlegm
el fuego – cold sore (herpes sore)
fumar – to smoke
    el cigarro / el cigarrillo – cigarette
    el puro – cigar
    la nicotina – nicotine
    el tabaco – tobacco
la gastritis – gastritis
la gingivitis – gingivitis
el hematoma (*masculino*) / el moretón – bruise
    el ojo morado – black eye
la hemorragia – hemorrhage
la hemorroide – hemorrhoid
la hepatitis – hepatitis
la herida – wound
herir (e → ie) (e → i) – to wound
el herpes – herpes
el hipo – (the) hiccups
hincharse – to become swollen / to swell (up)
la hinchazón – swelling
el hormigueo – tingling sensation
el infarto / el ataque al corazón – heart attack
la infección – infection
infectar – to infect
la inflamación – inflammation
la intoxicación alimentaria – food poisoning
intoxicado/a – (food) poisoned
el latido irregular del corazón – irregular heartbeat
latir – to beat (heart)
la llaga – sore
lastimar(se) – to hurt (oneself) / to get hurt
la lesión – injury
lesionar(se) – to injure (oneself)
el lunar – mole
maligno/a – malignant
la mancha – stain
manchar – to stain
la migraña / la jaqueca – migraine
mortal – mortal / fatal / deadly
el mal aliento – bad breath
el maltrato – mistreatment (usually physical abuse)
marearse – to get motion (sea) sick
el mareo – motion (sea) sickness
las náuseas – nausea
la neumonía / la pulmonía – pneumonia

el nivel – level
    los niveles altos – high levels
        de triglicéridos – high triglyceride levels
        de azúcar en la sangre – high blood sugar
ovular – to ovulate
la ovulación – ovulation
el parásito – parasite
el parto – childbirth / delivery
la presión de sangre – blood pressure
    la alta presión de sangre / la hipertensión
    la baja presión de sangre / la hipotensión
el pus – pus
quebrarse (e → ie) – to break (one's ____)
el quiste – cyst
la retinopatía – retinopathy
resbalar(se) – to slip accidentally
el riesgo – risk
    estar a riesgo (de) – to be at risk (of)
romperse – to break (one's ____) / to tear (one's ___)
roto/a – broken / torn
las ronchas – hives
salir (bien, mal) – to come/turn out (well, badly)
el salpullido / el sarpullido – rash
sangrar (el sangrado) – to bleed (bleeding – *noun*)
la sensación (de ardor) – (burning) sensation
el SIDA (síndrome de inmunodeficiencia adquirida) – AIDS
el síntoma (*masculino*) – symptom
el síndrome – syndrome
el SMSL (síndrome de la muerte súbita del lactante) – SIDS
la(s) sobredosis – overdose(s)
la somnolencia / la soñolencia – drowsiness
sordo/a (sordomudo/a) – deaf (deaf-mute)
súbito/a / repentino/a – sudden
sufrir (de) / padecer (c → zc) – to suffer (from)
el TEPT (trastorno de estrés postraumático) – PTSD
torcerse (o → ue) – to twist / to sprain (one's ____)
toser – to cough
el trastorno – disorder
el trauma (*masculino*) – trauma
la tuberculosis – tuberculosis
el tumor – tumor
la úlcera – ulcer
la varicela – chickenpox
la verruga – wart
el VIH (virus de la inmunodeficiencia humana) – HIV
    ser seropositivo/a – to be HIV positive
el VPH (virus del papiloma humano) – HPV
la violación – rape / violation
violar – to rape / to violate
viral – viral
el (los) virus – virus(es)
vomitar (los vómitos) – to vomit (vomiting – *noun*)
el vómito – vomit

preguntas básicas (tú)
¿Cómo te sientes? – How do you feel?
¿Cómo te encuentras? – How do you feel?
¿Qué te pasa? – What's going on (for you)?
¿Qué pasó? – What happened?
¿Qué te duele? – What hurts (you)?
¿Qué tienes? – What (symptoms) do you have?
¿Cómo te va? – How is it going (for you)?
¿Qué tal? – How are things?
¿Con qué frecuencia? – How often?

respuestas básicas
¡Ay! – Ouch! / Ow!
(a mí) me duele _____ – my _____ hurts
tener dolor de _____ – to have a _____ ache
tener / sentir (with *nouns*)
    calor – to be hot
    frío – to be cold
    fiebre / calentura – to have a fever
    gripe / gripa – to have the flu
    resfrío / resfriado – to have a cold
    tos – to have a cough
    problemas para + *inf.* – problems with ____ing
    dificultades para + *infinitivo* – difficulty ____ing
sentirse / encontrarse (with *adjectives* or *adverbs*)
    fatal – awful
    horrible / terrible – horrible / terrible
    resfriado/a – to have a cold
    (aun) mejor – (even) better
    (aun) peor – (even) worse
casi no – not really

la duración
¿Cuánto tiempo hace que tienes fiebre?
    – How long have you had a fever?
Hace dos días que tengo fiebre.
    – I have had a fever for two days.
Tengo fiebre desde hace dos días.
    – I have had a fever for two days.
He tenido fiebre por dos días.
    – I have had a fever for two days.
¿Cuánto tiempo hacía que tenías fiebre?
    – How long had you had a fever?
Hacía dos días que tenía fiebre.
    – I had had a fever for two days.
Tenía fiebre desde hacía dos días.
    – I had had a fever for two days.
Había tenido fiebre por dos días.
    – I had had a fever for two days.
por – for (duration of time)
todavía (no) – still / (not) yet
ya – already / now
ya no – not any more

para mejorarse o prevenir una enfermedad

el aborto – abortion
el agua oxigenada – hydrogen peroxide
el agua salada – salt water
la aguja – needle
la alternativa – alternative
amamantar / dar pecho – to breastfeed
el (los) análisis – analysis (analyses)
    de semen – semen analysis
la anestesia – anesthesia
anormal – abnormal
el antibiótico – antibiotic
el anticonceptivo – contraceptive
    el condón / el preservativo – condom
    "cuidar" (a la mujer) – (the) "pull-out" method
    el DIU (dispositivo intrauterino) – IUD
    el implante – implant
    la abstinencia (abstenerse) – abstinence
el antídoto – antidote
el antihistamínico – antihistamine
el aparato – piece of equipment / device
aplicar(se) / poner(se) – to apply / to put on (oneself)
el asilo para ancianos – retirement home
ayunar – to fast
    en ayunas – without breakfast / fasting
la báscula – scale (for weight)
la biopsia – biopsy
el catéter – catheter
el cepillo de dientes – toothbrush
cepillarse/lavarse los dientes – to brush one's teeth
la (operación) cesárea – cesarean section
chequear / checar – to check (to examine)
el chequeo – check (exam)
circuncidar – to circumcise
la circuncisión – circumcision
la cita / la consulta – appointment / consultation
la cirugía (plástica / estética) – (plastic) surgery
la clínica – clinic
la colonoscopia / la colonoscopía – colonoscopy
concertar (e → ie) – to arrange / to put together
concertar/hacer una cita – to make an appointment
el cuidado de (la) salud – healthcare
el cuidado paliativo – palliative care
el cuidado primario – primary care
cuidar(se) – to take care of (oneself)
la cura – (the) cure
curar – to cure
dar a luz (a) / aliviarse – to give birth (to)
dejar de + *infinitivo* – to quit _____ing
descansar – to rest
la diálisis – dialysis
la dieta – diet
    estar (ponerse) a dieta – to be (to go) on a diet

las grasas – fats
las proteínas – proteins
los carbohidratos – carbohydrates
digerir (e → ie) (e → i) – to digest
la digestión – digestion
el dispositivo – device
dormir (o → ue) (o → u) – to sleep
la(s) dosis – dose(s)
el empaste – (dental) filling
encasar (un hueso) – to set (a bone)
la epidural / la ráquea / la raquídea – epidural
el examen médico – medical exam
el (examen) físico – physical (exam)
examinar – to examine
el expediente / el historial clínico – medical chart
extirpar – to remove (surgically)
estéril – sterile
esterilizar – to sterilize
el estetoscopio – stethoscope
la farmacia / la droguería / la botica – pharmacy
los fármacos / las drogas – pharmaceuticals / drugs
el fluoruro – fluoride
la(s) gasa(s) – gauze
el glucómetro – glucometer
la gota – drop (of liquid) / gout
el hospital – hospital
el hábito – habit
    los hábitos alimenticios – eating habits
hacer gárgaras – to gargle
hacer preguntas – to ask questions
el hilo dental – dental floss
    usar el hilo dental – to floss
el inhalador (de rescate) – (rescue) inhaler
la histerectomía – hysterectomy
la incisión – incision
el IMC (índice de masa corporal) – BMI
intramuscular – intramuscular
intravenoso/a – intravenous
la inyección – injection
inyectar – to inject
el jarabe – (cough) syrup
la jeringa – syringe
el laboratorio – laboratory
la lactancia – lactation
la ligadura de trompas – tubal ligation
la mamografía – mammography / mammogram
el manicomio – mental hospital
mandar (a alguien a) – to send (someone to)
mandar (a) + *infinitivo* – to tell someone *to* _____
el medicamento – medication
    de mostrador – over-the-counter medication
la medicina / la droga – medicine / drug
mejorarse – to get better

el masaje – massage
monitorizar / monitorear – to monitor
la muestra – sample
    de orina – urine sample
    de heces / de materia fecal – stool sample
la pasta dental / la pasta dentífrica – toothpaste
la pastilla / la píldora / la tableta – pill / tablet
pinchar – to poke (with a needle) / to inject
la puntada / el punto de sutura – stitch
la operación – operation
operar – to operate
el orden (en orden) – order (in order / in place)
la orden – order (what was requested) / request
ordenar – to order / to request
prevenir (e → ie) – to prevent
priorizar – to prioritize
probar (o → ue) – to test
el procedimiento – procedure
proceder – to proceed
la prueba – test
    de sangre – blood test
quedarse en la cama – to stay in bed
la quimioterapia – chemotherapy
el quirófano – operating room (OR)
quirúrgico/a – surgical
la recuperación – recovery
recuperarse – to recover
la radiografía / los rayos equis – X-ray
la radioterapia – radiation therapy
la rehabilitación – rehabilitation
rehabilitar(se) – to rehabilitate (oneself)
la receta / la prescripción – prescription
el repuesto / el recambio – refill
respirar (inhalar, exhalar) – to breathe
resucitar – to resuscitate
el resultado – result
revivir – to revive / to relive
sacar sangre – to draw blood
la sala de emergencia – emergency room (ER/ED)
la sala de espera – waiting room
la sala de recuperación – recovery room
sanar(se) – to heal / to get better
el seguro / la aseguranza (médico/a) – insurance
el sexo (seguro) – (safe) sex
el seguimiento – follow-up
los signos vitales – vital signs
el sistema inmunológico – immune system
    "las defensas" – defenses
sobrio/a – sober
la sobriedad – sobriety
someterse (a) – to undergo / to subject oneself (to)
sonarse (o → ue) la nariz – to blow one's nose
la sonda – probe

el suero medicinal – IV fluids
suturar – to suture / to stitch
la temperatura – temperature
la terapia (del habla) – (speech) therapy
el termómetro – thermometer
la tira – strip
la tirita / la curita – adhesive bandage (Band Aid)
tomar – to take (by mouth) / to drink
tomar – to take (temperature, blood pressure, etc.)
tomar una decisión – to make a decision
el trasplante – transplant
el ultrasonido – ultrasound
la vasectomía – vasectomy
la vacuna – vaccine
vacunar (contra) – to vaccinate (against)
la venda – bandage
la venda adhesiva / la curita – adhesive bandage
vendar – to bandage
el yeso / la escayola – (plaster) cast

las posturas corporales y las expresiones faciales
acostarse (o → ue) – to lie down
acuclillarse – to squat down / to crouch down
    estar en cuclillas – to be crouching
asentir (e → ie) (e → i) con la cabeza – to nod
acurrucarse – to curl up / to snuggle up
agacharse – to duck down / to bend over
alzar / levantar (la cabeza) – to lift (one's head)
arrodillarse – to kneel down / to get on one's knees
bajar (la cabeza) – to lower (one's head)
boca abajo – upside down / face down
    prono/a – prone
boca arriba – right-side up / face up
    supino/a – supine
estar cabizbajo/a – to have one's head down (due
    to sadness, worry, embarrassment, dejection)
encogerse de hombros – to shrug one's shoulders
empinarse – to lean over / to bend over
erguirse (e → i) – to stand/sit up straight
    estar erguido/a – to be upright
fruncir el ceño – to frown
guiñar un ojo – to wink
hacer una mueca – to make a face
    la mueca – (funny) face / facial expression
levantarse – to get up
negar (e → ie) con la cabeza – to shake one's head no
ponerse de pie / pararse – to stand up
    estar de pie / estar parado/a – to be standing
    estar de puntillas – to be on one's tippy-toes
señalar con el dedo / apuntar – to point
sentarse (e → i) – to sit down / to sit up
    estar sentado/a – to be seated / to be sitting
sonreír (e → í) (e →) – to smile

los ejercicios y los estiramientos
hacer – to do
    (los) abdominales – situps / crunches
    (las) dominadas – pullups
    (las) lagartijas / (las) flexiones – pushups
    (los) marineros – jumping jacks
    (las) sentadillas – squats
levantar pesas – to lift weights
montar en bicicleta – to ride a bicycle
nadar – to swim
caminar – to walk
    salir a caminar / ir a pasear – to go for a walk
estirarse – to stretch
saltar / brincar – to jump / to bounce
manejar (el estrés, etc.) – to manage (stress, etc.)

los títulos profesionales
el / la anestesiólogo/a – anesthesiologist
el / la asistente/a médico/a – medical assistant (MA)
el / la asociado/a médico/a – physician assistant (PA)
el / la cardiólogo/a – cardiologist
el / la consejero/a – counselor / advisor
el / la cirujano/a – surgeon
    ortopédico/a – orthopedic surgeon
el / la dentista – dentist
el / la dermatólogo/a – dermatologist
el / la dietista / nutricionista – dietitian / nutritionist
el / la encargado/a – (the) person in charge
el / la enfermero/a (practicante/a) – nurse (practitioner)
el / la especialista (en) – specialist (in)
el / la farmacéutico/a / farmaceuta – pharmacist
el / la gastroenterólogo/a – gastroenterologist
el / la gineco-obstetra – OB/GYN
    el / la ginecólogo/a – gynecologist
    el / la obstetra – obstetrician
el / la intérprete – interpreter (verbal)
el / la masajista – massage therapist
el / la médico/a – medical doctor (MD)
el / la neumólogo/a – pulmonologist
el / la neurólogo/a – neurologist
el / la optometrista – optometrist
el / la oncólogo/a – oncologist
el / la ortodoncista – orthodontist
el / la ortopedista – orthopedist
el / la pediatra – pediatrician
el / la proveedor/a – provider
el / la psicólogo/a – psychologist
el / la psiquiatra – psychiatrist
el / la quiropráctico/a – chiropractor
el / la radiólogo/a – radiologist
el / la terapeuta / terapista – therapist
el / la traductor/a – translator (written)
el / la urólogo/a – urologist

otras palabras y expresiones útiles
lo antes posible / tan pronto (como sea) posible /
    lo más pronto posible / cuanto antes
        – as soon as possible
como mucho – at (the) most
como pronto – at the earliest
como tarde / a más tardar – at the latest
bilingüe – bilingual
trilingüe – trilingual
cuatrilingüe – quadrilingual
multilingüe – multilingual
tutear / tratar a alguien de "tú" – to speak to
    someone as "tú"
ustedear / tratar a alguien de "Ud." – to speak to
    someone as "usted"
de parte de (de mi parte) – on behalf of
la razón de (la cita) – (the) reason for (the appt.)
de hecho – in fact / actually
actualmente – currently
actualizar – to update
disponible – available
la disponibilidad – availability
el testamento vital – living will
la voluntad anticipada – advance directives
estar atento/a a la llamada – to be on call
confidencial – confidential
la confidencialidad – confidentiality
consentir (e → ie) (e → i) – to consent
el consentimiento – consent
lamentar – to regret
lamentablemente – regrettably
¿A ver? – Let me see?
A ver … – Let's see …
o sea / es decir – that is to say (clarification)
mejor dicho / más bien – rather (slight correction)
evidentemente – evidently
efectivamente – effectively
aparentemente / por lo visto – apparently
¿A nombre de quién? – Under what name?
a nombre de _____ – under (name)
el milagro – miracle
bendecir (e → i) – to bless
bendito/a – blessed
la bendición – blessing
maldecir (e → i) – to curse
maldito/a – cursed / damned
la maldición – curse
el formulario / la forma – form
    llenar – to fill out
    la casilla – check box
    la marca de verificación/visto – checkmark
    firmar – to sign (one's name)
el costado – side (of the body or any solid object)

Unidad 26 – la vida doméstica

las viviendas / el alojamiento – housing
el apartamento / el departamento – apartment
la casa – house
la casa de remolque – mobile home
el parque de remolques – mobile home park
el condominio – condominium
la hipoteca – mortgage
el hogar – home / hearth
alojar / hospedar – to host / to put (someone) up
alojarse / hospedarse / quedarse (en) – to stay (at)
el / la huésped/a – guest (overnight)
el / la invitado/a – guest (for the day)
recibir / acoger – to welcome (to one's home)
estar/ser bienvenido/a – to be welcome
dar la bienvenida – to welcome
la (cordial / cálida) acogida – (warm) welcome
acogedor/a – welcoming

la vivienda – dwelling
el balcón – balcony
el (cuarto de) baño / el servicio – bathroom
el camino particular – driveway
la casa (de ____ pisos) – (____ story) house
la cocina – kitchen
el comedor – dining room
el cuarto (de huéspedes) – (guest) room
el desván / el ático / el altillo / el entretecho – attic
el dormitorio / la habitación / la recámara / la alcoba – bedroom
la entrada – entryway / entrance
la(s) escalera(s) – stairs / staircase
   escaleras abajo – downstairs
   escaleras arriba – upstairs
el estudio – studio / study
el frente – (the) front
el fondo – (the) bottom / (the) back / background
el garaje / la cochera – garage / carport
el jardín – yard
el lavadero – laundry room
la pared / el muro – wall
el patio – patio
el (primer) piso – (first) floor
   de madera – wood floor (wooden)
   de azulejo – tile floor
el porche – porch
el portal – entryway / front door
la sala / el living – living room
la sala de estar – family room
el sótano – basement
el suelo – ground / floor (not numbered)
el taller – workshop

el techo / el cielo – ceiling
el tejado / el techo – roof
la ventana – window

las cosas de la casa o del jardín
la alfombra – carpet
la almohada – (bed) pillow
el árbol – tree
   el arce – maple tree
   el manzano – apple tree
   el naranjo – orange tree
   el olmo – elm tree
   el peral – pear tree
   el pino – pine tree
   el roble – oak tree
el arbusto – bush
   el rosal – rosebush
el banco / la banca – bench
la bañera / la tina – bathtub
la cama / el lecho – bed
el cartel / el póster, *pl.* los pósters – poster(s)
el cerco / la cerca – fence
el césped / el sacate (zacate) – lawn
la chimenea – fireplace / chimney
los cobertores – (the) covers
la cobija / la manta – blanket
la colcha / el cubrecama(s) – comforter / bedspread
el colchón – mattress
el cojín – throw pillow / couch cushion
la cómoda – dresser
la cortina – curtain
las cosas – things / stuff
el cuadro – picture (usually framed)
la ducha – shower
el electrodoméstico – electrical appliance
el escritorio – desk
el espejo – mirror
el estéreo – stereo
   la bocina / el parlante / el altavoz – speaker
el estante – shelf / bookcase
la estantería – bookcase / shelving
la estufa – stove
el fregadero – kitchen sink
el guardarropa / el clóset / el armario – closet
el horno (de microondas) – (microwave) oven
el huerto – garden
el inodoro / el retrete / la taza – toilet (bowl)
la lámpara – lamp
el lavabo / el (los) lavamanos – bathroom sink(s)
la lavadora – washing machine
el (los) lavaplatos – dishwasher(s)

la llave / el grifo – faucet
el mantel – tablecloth
la mecedora – rocking chair
la mesa – table
el mostrador – counter / countertop
el mueble – piece of furniture
la plancha – iron
la plomería – plumbing
la puerta – door
    la bisagra – hinge
    el dintel – doorway / doorjamb
    el picaporte – doorknocker / door handle
    el pomo – doorknob
    la manija / la manilla – door handle
    la cadena – chain
    la cerradura – lock
    entreabierto/a – halfway open
    abierto/a de par en par – wide open
el refrigerador (refri) / el frigorífico / la nevera
    – refrigerator (fridge)
el reloj – clock / watch
la repisa – mantelpiece / windowsill / shelf
    el alféizar / la alfeiza – ledge / windowsill
la sábana – bed sheet
el (los) salvamanteles – placemat(s) / coaster(s)
la secadora – (clothes) dryer
la silla – chair
el sillón, *pl.* los sillones – arm chair(s)
el sofá (*masculino*) – couch / sofa
el tapete – rug
el televisor – TV set
hacer juego con – to go with / to match

las herramientas y la ferretería

los alicates – plyers
la arandela – washer
el azadón – hoe
la cinta (adhesiva) – (sticky / adhesive) tape
el clavo – nail
el contenedor / el recipiente – container
el (los) cortacésped – lawnmower(s)
el cubo / el balde – bucket / pail
el destapador de inodoros / el amigo – toilet plunger
el destornillador – screwdriver
la escoba – broom
la ferretería – hardware / hardware store
el flexómetro / la cinta métrica – tape measure
la fregona / el trapeador – mop
la herramienta – tool
el rastrillo – rake
la lima – file
la llave – key
la llave inglesa – wrench
la manguera – (garden) hose

el martillo – hammer
la pala – shovel
el papel de lija – sandpaper
la tachuela – tack / pushpin
las tijeras – scissors
el tornillo – screw / bolt
la tuerca – nut

las descripciones

antiguo/a – antique / old
áspero/a – rough (surface)
bastante – quite / rather (*adverb*)
bastante / suficiente – enough (*adjective*)
blando/a / suave – soft
confortable / cómodo/a – comfortable
cuadrado/a – square
de cuero – (made of) leather
de madera – wooden / (made of) wood
de metal – (made of) metal
de tela – (made of) cloth
de mala calidad / chafa – low quality
de buena calidad – high quality
duro/a – hard
incómodo/a – uncomfortable
limpio/a – clean
liso/a – smooth (surface)
mugriento/a / sucio/a – filthy / dirty
    la mugre / la suciedad – filth / dirtiness
ovalado/a – oval (shaped)
plano/a – flat (surface)
redondo/a – round
delantero/a – front
trasero/a – back

los quehaceres y otras acciones

abrir la llave/el agua – to turn on the water
abrir la puerta con llave – to unlock the door
alimentar / dar de comer – to feed
apretar (e → ie) – to tighten / to squeeze
arar – to plow
arreglar – to tidy up / to fix
barrer – to sweep
cerrar la llave/el agua – to turn off the water
cerrar la puerta con llave – to lock the door
cocinar / cocer (o → ue) (c → z) – to cook
coser – to sew
colgar (o → ue) – to hang (up)
cortar (el césped) – to cut / to mow (the lawn)
criar (i → í) niños – to raise kids
el deber doméstico – domestic duty
doblar / plegar (e → ie) – to fold
desempolvar – to dust
empapar – to soak
excavar – to dig

fregar (e → ie) / trapear – to mop
fregar – to scrub
guardar – to put away / to keep
hacer la cama – to make the bed
lavar – to wash
lijar – to sand
limar – to file (down)
limpiar – to clean (up)
martillar / clavar – to hammer
mojar – to wet
mover con pala – to shovel
pasar la aspiradora / aspirar – to vacuum
pasar un trapo – to wipe (with a rag)
planchar – to iron
poner / colocar – to put / to place / to set
preparar – to prepare
pulir – to polish
el quehacer (de la casa) – (household) chore
quitar – to clear off / to remove (from surface)
rastrillar (las hojas) – to rake (the leaves)
recoger – to pick up / to straighten up
regar (e → ie) – to water
reparar – to repair / to fix
rociar (i → í) – to spray
sacar – to take out / to remove (from within)
sacudir – to shake
secar – to dry
soler (o → ue) + *inf.* – to be in the habit of _____*ing*
tejer – to knit
tender (e → ie) – to lay out / to stretch out
tender a + *infinitivo* – to tend *to* _____
tocar/llamar a la puerta – to knock on the door
la fuerza – strength
la debilidad – weakness
el punto débil – weakness / weak point
el punto fuerte – strength / strong point

el coche / el carro / el auto – car / automobile
la motocicleta (moto) – motorcycle
el / la motociclista / motorista – motorcyclist / biker
el monovolumen – minivan
el camión – truck (general)
la troca – pickup (truck)
el / la conductor/a – driver
conducir (c → zc) / manejar – to drive
el volante – steering wheel
arrancar el carro – to start the car
el arranque – ignition
la batería – (car) battery
el salpicadero – dashboard
la guantera – glovebox
el (los) parabrisas – windshield(s)
el (los) limpiaparabrisas – windshield wiper(s)

el foco – headlight
el asiento – seat
el respaldo – backrest
la cajuela / el maletero – trunk
la defensa / el (los) parachoques – bumper(s)
el motor – engine
la transmisión – transmission
el espejo retrovisor – rearview mirror
    el ángulo muerto – blind spot
el intermitente / la flecha – blinker
la velocidad – speed / gear
la palanca – gearshift
el pedal – pedal
    el acelerador – accelerator / gas pedal
    el freno – brake
    el embrague – clutch
el velocímetro – speedometer
la llanta – tire
la rueda – wheel
el escape – exhaust pipe / tailpipe
la gasolina – gasoline
el gasóleo – diesel fuel
el tanque / el depósito – gas tank
el aceite / el óleo (de motor) – (motor) oil
adelantar – to go ahead (of) / to pass
estacionar / parquear / aparcar – to park
    el estacionamiento / el aparcamiento – parking lot
descomponerse / estropearse – to break down
la grúa – tow truck / crane
remolcar – to tow
atropellar – to run over
estallar / explotar – to explode
chocar / estrellarse (con / contra) – to crash (into)

otras palabras y expresiones útiles
el ama de casa (*femenino*) – homemaker / housewife
bajar – to go down / to lower
subir – to go up / to raise
abajo – below / down
arriba – above / up
el chisme – gossip
chismear – to gossip
el / la chismoso/a – one who gossips
el / la criado/a – housekeeper / nanny
de otra manera – otherwise
hay – there is / there are
había – there was / there were
hay que + *infinitivo* – one has *to* _____
había que + *infinitivo* – one had *to* _____
haber de + *infinitivo* – to have *to* _____
    Hubo de hacerlo. – He had to do it.
¿Qué hay (de nuevo)? – What's new?
¿Qué hubo(le)? – What's new?

Unidad 27 – las ciencias y la tecnología

la física – physics
la astrofísica – astrophysics
    la astronomía – astronomy
    el espacio exterior – outer space
    el agujero negro – black hole
    la rotación – rotation
    rotar – to rotate
    girar – to spin / to turn
    alrededor (de) / en torno (a) – around
    la órbita – orbit
    el eje – axis
    la trayectoria – trajectory
físico/a – physical
la masa – mass
la velocidad – velocity / speed
acelerar – to accelerate
la aceleración – acceleration
la gravedad – gravity
la fuerza de gravedad – gravitational force
el momento – momentum
la inercia – inertia
el volumen – volume
la capacidad – capacity
la magnitud – magnitude
el campo – field
electromagnético/a – electromagnetic
magnético/a – magnetic
el magnetismo – magnetism
el imán – magnet
la acción – action
la reacción nuclear – nuclear reaction
térmico/a – thermal
atómico/a – atomic
el átomo – atom
    el electrón – electron
    el protón – proton
    el neutrón – neutron
el ion – ion
la carga – charge
eléctrico/a – electrical
negativo/a – negative
positivo/a – positive
neutro/a – neutral
la partícula – particle
el núcleo – nucleus
la fusión nuclear – nuclear fusion
la fisión nuclear – nuclear fission
radioactivo/a / radiactivo/a – radioactive
la energía – energy
potencial – potential
cinético/a – kinetic

la química – chemistry
la bioquímica – biochemistry
    el ADN (ácido desoxirribonucleico) – DNA
    la hormona – hormone
    el metabolismo – metabolism
la materia – matter
el estado – state of being
el sólido (sólido/a) – solid
el líquido (líquido/a) – liquid
el gas (gaseoso/a) – gas (gaseous)
el plasma (*masculino*) – plasma
    plasmático/a – plasmatic / plasma
la reacción química – chemical reaction
el enlace químico – chemical bond
    el enlace covalente – covalent bond
    el enlace iónico – ionic bond
el químico (químico/a) – chemical
la molécula – molecule
el elemento – element
el compuesto (compuesto/a) – compound
la tabla periódica de los elementos – periodic table
                                 of elements

la biología – biology
la microbiología – microbiology
la taxonomía – taxonomy
agrupar – to group (together)
el dominio – domain
    el reino – kingdom
    el filo / la división – phylum
    la clase – class
    el orden – order
    la familia – family
    el género – genus
    la especie – species
la nomenclatura – nomenclature
    binomial – binomial nomenclature
la evolución – evolution
evolucionar – to evolve
la filogenia – phylogeny
adaptarse (a) – to adapt (to)
la mutación – mutation
mutante – mutant
complejo/a – complex
el ser (vivo, humano) – (living, human) being
el organismo – organism
el gen – gene
la genética – genetics
genético/a – genetic
sobrevivir (a) – to survive
la sobrevivencia / la supervivencia – survival
el / la sobreviviente / superviviente – survivor

la electricidad – electricity

el amperio – ampere
la corriente – current
    eléctrica – electrical current
    alterna – alternating current (AC)
    continua – direct current (DC)
el circuito – circuit
el corto circuito – short circuit
la potencia / el potencial – power
el voltaje – voltage
el voltio – volt
el vataje – wattage
el vatio – watt

la tecnología – technology

el telescopio – telescope
el microscopio – microscope
los (anteojos) prismáticos – binoculars
la lupa – magnifying glass
el alcoholímetro – breathalyzer
el altímetro – altimeter
el velocímetro – speedometer
la máquina – machine
el (teléfono) celular (celu) / el móvil – cell / mobile
la tableta / la tablet – tablet
la informática / la computación – computing
la base de datos – database
los datos – data
la computadora (compu) / el ordenador – computer
la fuente de alimentación – power supply
iniciar – to start / to boot up (app, computer, etc.)
reiniciar – to restart / to reboot
el procesador – processor
el hardware – hardware
el disco duro – hard drive
la memoria – memory
el equipo – (computer) equipment
el estuche / la funda – (carrying, protective) case
el router – router
el módem – modem
el software – software
la pantalla (táctil) – (touch) screen
el teclado (táctil) – (touch) keyboard
la tecla – key (of a keyboard)
la impresora – printer
imprimir – to print
el ratón (táctil) – mouse (touch pad)
el micrófono – microphone
electrónico/a – electronic
el alambre – wire
inalámbrico/a – wireless
el tomacorriente – surge protector
la clavija – power plug

el enchufe – power outlet
enchufar – to plug in
el cable – cable / cord
    de extensión – extension cord
la pila – battery
el cargador – charger
cargar – to charge / to load
sobrecargar – to overload
avanzado/a – advanced
avanzar – to advance
el avance / el adelanto – advancement
progresar – to progress
el progreso – progress
obsoleto/a – obsolete
el paso – step
la etapa – stage (of a process)
la pauta – guideline
la manera / la forma – (the) way
la posibilidad – possibility
el proceso – process
procesar – to process
actual / corriente – current (time)
actualmente – currently
hoy en día – nowadays
reciente – recent
recién / recientemente – recently
últimamente – lately
la iluminación – lighting / illumination
la calefacción – heating
el aire acondicionado – air conditioning
central – central
la temperatura ambiente – room temperature
la novedad – novelty
el transformador – transformer
el fusible – fuse
el interruptor – light switch / power switch
el conductor – conductor
la bombilla – lightbulb
el adaptador – adapter
la conexión – connection
conectar – to connect
convertir (e → ie) (e → i) (en) – to convert (to)
descubrir – to discover / to uncover
el descubrimiento – discovery
inventar – to invent
la invención / el invento – invention
ocupar – to occupy
el modelo – model / template
sonar (o → ue) (a) – to sound (like) / to ring
caber (yo quepo) – to fit (inside)
técnico/a – technical
el programa (*masculino*) – program
programar – to program / to schedule

los medios de comunicación social – social media

la red social – social network
la red – network / (the) internet / (the) net
el (la) internet – (the) internet / (the) web
el dominio – domain
la plataforma – platform
el sitio web – website
la página web – web page
en línea – online
hacer clic (izquierdo, derecho) – to (left, right) click
arrastrar – to drag
guardar – to save
cortar, copiar, pegar – to cut, to copy, to paste
surfear / navegar – to surf / to navigate
el buscador – search engine
buscar – to search (for)
la búsqueda / la busca – search
en busca/búsqueda de – in search of
la aplicación / la app – application / app
googlear – to google
el foro / el fórum – forum
el chat – chat (digital)
chatear – to chat (digitally)
el texto – text
textear – to text
mandar / enviar (i → í) – to send
el correo electrónico – email
el / la remitente – sender
el / la destinatario/a – recipient
la bandeja de entrada – inbox
el mensaje / el recado – message
dejar un recado – to leave a message
tuitear – to tweet
el tuit – tweet
el perfil – profile
la contraseña – password
el nombre de usuario – user name
el / la usuario/a – user
la clave – key / passcode
acceder (a) – to access
el wifi – WiFi
la cobertura – coverage
cubrir – to cover
la captura de pantalla – screenshot
el vínculo / el enlace – link
por defecto – by default
el promedio – average
funcionar – to work / to function
servir (e → i) – to work / to function
servir (de) – to serve (as)
el / la nómada digital – digital nomad
la prensa – (the) press
las noticias – (the) news

otras palabras y expresiones útiles

junto a – next to
junto con – along with
cada cual / cada uno – each one (thing)
cada quien / cada uno – each one (person)
alguno/a que otro/a _____
    – an occasional _____ (here and there)
para colmo – to top it all off
yo, a mi vez (ella, a su vez) – I, in turn (she, in turn)
asimismo / también – also / too
específico/a – specific
de hecho – actually / in fact
a medida que – as
proponer – to propose
la propuesta – proposal
la subvención – (monetary) grant
la patente de invención – patent
el premio – award / prize
el cumplido – compliment
el halago / la alabanza / el elogio – praise / flattery
halagar / alabar / elogiar – to praise / to flatter
agradar / complacer (c → zc) – to please
agradable – pleasant / pleasing
desagradable – unpleasant
favorable – favorable
la mayoría – (the) majority
la minoría – (the) minority
el consenso – consensus
científico/a – scientific
el método – method
observar – to observe
la(s) hipótesis – hypothesis (hypotheses)
el experimento – experiment
el estudio – study
controlar – to control
repetir (e → i) – to repeat
el objetivo – objective
comprobar (o → ue) – to prove
rechazar – to reject
aceptar – to accept
colaborar – to collaborate
confirmar – to confirm
el esfuerzo – effort / endeavor
aumentar – to increase / to raise
disminuir (y) – to decrease / to diminish
la esperanza – hope
ampliar (i → í) / expandir – to broaden / to expand
extender (e → ie) – to extend
adepto/a – adept
inepto/a – inept
el conocimiento – knowledge
la sabiduría – wisdom
sabio/a – wise

Unidad 28 – el crimen, las delincuencias y la justicia

los crímenes y las delincuencias
el crimen – crime (serious crime, like murder)
la delincuencia – delincuency (generic crime)
el delito – crime (less serious than *crimen*)
el / la delincuente – delinquent / criminal
el / la criminal – criminal
la violencia – violence
el terrorismo – terrorism
el / la terrorista – terrorist
robar – to rob / to steal
a mano armada – at gunpoint
el ladrón / la ladrona – thief
disparar / tirar – to shoot
a quemarropa – at point-blank range
golpear / pegar – to hit
a palos – with sticks or clubs (bludgeon)
a puñetazos – by punching / with (his/her) fists
asesinar – to assassinate / to murder
el asesinato – assassination
matar – to kill
la matanza – killing
a puñaladas – by stabbing
apuñalar – to stab
el / la asesino/a – assassin / murderer
el / la sicario/a – hitman / hitwoman
el tiroteo – shootout
la masacre – massacre
el atentado / el ataque – attack
asaltar / atacar – to assault / to attack
lidiar / pelear / luchar – to fight / to struggle
dañar / hacer daño (a) – to damage / to harm
destruir (y) / destrozar – to destroy
recurrir (a) – to resort (to)
la pandilla – gang
el / la pandillero/a – gang member
el / la secuestrador/a – kidnapper
secuestrar / raptar – to kidnap
el secuestro – kidnapping
linchar – to lynch
provocar – to provoke
incitar – to incite
el motín – riot
la huelga – strike
la protesta / la manifestación – protest
acosar – to harass
el acoso (sexual) – (sexual) harassment
hubo (haber) – there was/were (used for events)
había (haber) – there was/were (describes scene)
el narcotráfico – drug trafficking
el / la narcotraficante – drug dealer
la mula / el burro – drug mule

el contrabando – contraband
la cocaína – cocaine
la heroína – heroin
la marihuana / la mota – marijuana / pot
la jerga / el argot – jargon / slang
estafar – to cheat / to swindle
el / la estafador/a – cheater / swindler
chantajear / extorsionar – to blackmail / to extort
el chantaje / la extorsión – blackmail / extortion
sobornar – to bribe
el soborno / la mordida – bribe
el soplón / la soplona – snitch / rat / whistleblower
soplar – to snitch / to rat out / to blow the whistle
el / la cabeza de turco – fall guy
el chivo expiatorio – scapegoat
el / la cómplice – accomplice
denunciar – to turn in / to report / to denounce
la venganza – revenge / retribution
entregarse / rendirse – to turn oneself in / to surrender
el arma (*femenino*), *pl.* las armas – weapon(s)
el arma de fuego – firearm
armar – to arm / to assemble / to put together
la bomba (explosiva) – bomb
explotar / estallar / explosionar – to explode
el explosivo – explosive
hacer explotar / detonar – to set off / to detonate
la navaja / el cuchillo / el arma blanca – knife
la pistola – pistol
la ametralladora – machine gun
el rifle – rifle
la escopeta – shotgun
el casquillo – bullet shell
la bala – bullet
   (el chaleco) antibala – bulletproof (vest)
la guerra – war
la paz – peace

el lugar de los hechos – crime scene
la víctima – victim (regardless of gender or sex)
resultar – to become (injured, wounded, etc.)
herido/a – wounded
ileso/a – uninjured
sano/a y salvo/a – safe and sound
estar a salvo – to be safe
la precaución – precaution
morir (o → ue) (o → u) / fallecer (c → zc) – to die
el / la muerto/a / difunto/a – dead person
el cadáver – dead body
la cuestión de vida o muerte – matter of life or death
el / la paramédico/a – paramedic
los primeros auxilios – first aid

resucitar / revivir / volver a la vida – to resuscitate
la ambulancia – ambulance
las urgencias – (the) emergency room (ER/ED)
investigar – to investigate
el / la detective – detective
la policía (poli) – (the) police / police force
el / la policía (poli) – police officer
arrestar – to arrest
detener (e → ie) – to detain
clandestino/a – undercover
la patrulla – patrol car / squad car
la fuerza de tarea (antidroga) – (anti-drug) task force
perseguir (e → i) – to chase / to pursue
el / la sospechoso/a – suspect
sospechoso/a – suspicious
evitar / evadir – to avoid / to evade
huir (y) – to flee
dirigirse (a) – to head in a direction
dirigir – to direct
esconder(se) / ocultar(se) – to hide (oneself)
cazar – to hunt
la caza – hunt / manhunt
el / la cazador/a de recompensas – bounty hunter
suceder / ocurrir – to happen / to occur
el suceso / el evento / el acontecimiento – event
el suicidio – suicide
suicidarse – to commit suicide
el / la rehén, *pl.* los / las rehenes – hostage(s)
arriesgar / poner a riesgo (de) – to (put at) risk (of)
correr el riesgo (de) – to run the risk (of)
asombrar – to amaze / to astonish
espantar / asustar – to scare
preocuparse (de) – to worry / to get worried (about)
temer – to fear
el temor / el miedo – fear
rescatar / salvar – to rescue / to save
el rescate – rescue
alarmar – to alarm
entrar en acción / actuar (u → ú) – to act

el sistema de justicia criminal
bajo custodia – in custody
el / la reo/a – defendant / prisoner / accused
enfrentar cargos – to face charges
el derecho (a) – (the) right (to)
legal – legal
ilegal – illegal
justo/a – fair / just
injusto/a – unfair / unjust
la justicia – justice
el / la abogado/a – lawyer / attorney
el / la juez/a, *pl.* los / las jueces/zas – judge(s)
el jurado – jury

el / la jurado/a – juror
el tribunal – courtroom / court
el juzgado / la corte – courthouse / court
la ley – (the) law
confiscar / decomisar – to confiscate / to seize
la orden de alejamiento – restraining order
el toque de queda – curfew
el hecho – fact
identificar – to identify
el / la testigo – witness
atestiguar / testificar – to testify
la evidencia – evidence
defender (e → ie) – to defend
la autodefensa / la defensa propia – self-defense
ser inocente – to be innocent
ser culpable – to be guilty
la culpa – blame
culpar / acusar – to blame / to accuse
el / la acusado/a – the accused
llegar a un acuerdo – to reach an agreement
el fallo – ruling / judgment
poner en libertad – to release / to set free
librar / liberar – to free
ser libre – to be free (not detained)
la sentencia / la condena – sentence
sentenciar / condenar – to sentence / to condemn
imponer – to impose
la medida – measure / action
meter en la cárcel / encarcelar – to (put in) jail
la cárcel / la prisión – jail / prison
el bote – (the) joint / (the) pen / (the) slammer
la cadena perpetua – life sentence
la pena de muerte – (the) death penalty
el / la prisionero/a / preso/a – prisoner
severo/a – severe
la multa – fine
castigar – to punish
el castigo – punishment
arrepentirse (e → ie) (e → i) (de) – to repent / to regret
reformar(se) – to reform (to become reformed)
superar – to overcome / to surpass
acabar (con) – to end / to put an end (to)
el fracaso / el fallo – failure
fracasar / fallar – to fail
sorprendente – surprising
el tipo – type / kind / kind of person
demandar – to sue / to demand
la demanda – lawsuit / demand
la deuda – debt
contratar – to contract / to hire
el / la (los / las) guardaespaldas – bodyguard(s)
el / la guardia – guard
vigilar – to watch over (something / someone)

Unidad 29 – la política y los asuntos mundiales

el gobierno – (the) government
    federal – (the) federal government
    estatal – (the) state government
el / la gobernador/a – governor
el gabinete – cabinet
gobernar (e → ie) – to govern
gubernamental – governmental
la constitución – constitution
la separación de poderes – separation of powers
la rama – branch
    judicial – judicial branch
    legislativa – legislative branch
    ejecutiva – executive branch
el distrito – district
el congreso – congress
el / la congresista – member of congress
el / la diputado/a / representante – representative
el senado – senate
el / la senador/a – senator
la presidencia – presidency
el / la presidente/a – president
el / la vicepresidente/a – vice president
el / la secretario/a – secretary
    de la Defensa – Secretary of Defense
    del Estado – Secretary of State
    del Tesoro – Secretary of the Treasury
la Primera Dama – First Lady
el / la primer/a ministro/a – prime minister
el parlamento – parliament

la política – politics / policy
el / la político/a – politician / political
el partido (político) – (political) party
el / la aliado/a – ally / allied
el comunismo – communism
comunista – communist
el socialismo – socialism
socialista – socialist
la democracia – democracy
el / la demócrata – democrat
democrático/a – democratic
la república – republic
republicano/a – republican
el fascismo – fascism
fascista – fascist
conservador/a – conservative
liberal – liberal
las elecciones – (the) election / elections
libre – free
corrupto/a – corrupt
la corrupción – corruption

el fraude – fraud
fraudulento/a – fraudulent
la revolución – revolution
revolucionario/a – revolutionary
la protesta / la manifestación – protest
la marcha – march
marchar(se) – to march / to leave
la dictadura – dictatorship
el / la dictador/a – dictator
la tiranía – tyranny
el / la tirano/a – tyrant
tiránico/a – tyrannical
las represalias – reprisal / retaliation
la diplomacia – diplomacy
el / la diplomático/a – diplomat / diplomatic
las Naciones Unidas – (the) United Nations
la Unión Europea – (the) European Union
la OTAN – NATO
la OPEP – OPEC
el tratado de libre comercio – free-trade agreement
la campaña (electoral) – (electoral) campaign
postularse / lanzarse (para) – to run (for) (office)
el / la candidato/a – candidate
la candidatura – candidacy
prometer – to promise
la promesa – promise
implicar – to implicate / to imply
convencer (c → z) – to convince
el debate – debate
debatir – to debate
el / la rival – rival
vencer (c → z) / derrotar – to defeat
elegir (e → i) – to elect / to choose
votar (por) – to vote (for)
el voto – vote / ballot
la urna – ballot box
el / la ciudadano/a – citizen
indocumentado/a – undocumented
la frontera (política) – (political) border
el muro – wall
la inmigración – immigration
la redada – raid
deportar – to deport
la visa / el visado – visa
el asilo político – political asylum
la ley – law
justo/a – fair
la justicia – justice
injusto/a – unfair
la injusticia – injustice
el ambiente / el entorno – environment

la(s) crisis – crisis (crises)

el tornado – tornado
el huracán – hurricane
el deslave – mudslide / landslide
el terremoto / el seísmo / el sismo – earthquake
el maremoto – earthquake at sea
el temblor – tremor
la nevada – snowfall
la inundación – flood
el apagón – blackout
escaso/a – scarce
la escasez – scarcity / shortage
la sequía – drought
la hambruna – famine
morir(se) de hambre – to starve
la tormenta (eléctrica) – (electrical) storm
el relámpago – lightning
el trueno – thunder
el rayo (cayó) – lightning bolt (struck)
el incendio – fire
la Cruz Roja – (the) Red Cross
humanitario/a – humanitarian
voluntario/a – voluntary
el auxilio / el socorro / el amparo – aid / help
¡Auxilio! / ¡Socorro! – Help!
huir (y) – to flee
el / la refugiado/a – refugee
el refugio – refuge / shelter
sin hogar / sin techo – homeless
el / la mendigo/a – beggar
rogar (o → ue) / suplicar / mendigar – to beg
desamparado/a – helpless / uncared-for
abandonar – to abandon
abandonado/a – abandoned
necesitado/a – needy
vulnerable – vulnerable
entrar en pánico / sentir pánico – to panic
el / la huérfano/a – orphan
el orfanato / el orfanatorio – orphanage
anciano/a – elderly
jubilado/a – retired
jubilarse / retirarse – to retire
los servicios sociales – social services
el seguro social – social security
minusválido/a – handicapped
la minusvalía – handicap
discapacitado/a – disabled
la discapacidad – disability
cojo/a – lame (has a limp) / one-legged
manco/a – one-handed (missing a hand)
tuerto/a – one-eyed (missing an eye)
ciego/a – blind
sordo/a (sordomudo/a) – deaf (deaf-mute)
paralizado/a – paralyzed

las fuerzas armadas – (the) armed forces

el ejército – (the) army
la fuerza aérea – (the) air force
la marina de guerra – (the) navy / (the) marines
la guardia nacional – (the) national guard
militar – military (*adjective*)
el / la marinero/a – sailor / marine
el / la soldado – soldier
alistarse / inscribirse (en) – to enlist / to sign up
la inscripción – enlistment / registration
reclutar – to recruit
la conscripción – (the) draft / military service
el rango – rank
el / la sargento – sergeant
el / la general – general
el / la teniente/a – lieutenant
el capitán / la capitana – captain
el / la coronel – colonel
el / la almirante – admiral
el / la comandante – commandant / commander
el regimiento – regiment
las tropas – troops
mandar – to order / to send
la batalla – battle
batallar – to battle
la guerra – war
la carne de cañón – cannon fodder
la metralla – shrapnel
la granada – grenade
la ametralladora – machine gun
el arma (*femenino*) – weapon
    nuclear – nuclear weapon
    biológica – biological weapon
aniquilar – to annihilate
invadir – to invade
apoderarse (de) / ocupar – to take control (of)
saquear – to plunder / to pillage / to loot
el recurso natural – natural resource
el petróleo – oil / petroleum
el diamante – diamond
el platino – platinum
el acero – steel
expandir – to expand
la expansión – expansion
escoltar – to escort / to guard / to protect
el golpe de Estado – coup d'État
impedir (e → i) – to impede
contener (e → ie) – to contain
obtener (e → ie) – to obtain
encontrar (o → ue) / hallar – to find
realizar – to carry out / to realize (a dream)
llevar a cabo – to carry out / to make happen
la consecuencia – consequence
la repercusión – repercussion

la economía – (the) economy
económico/a – economic / economical
la huelga / el paro – strike
el desempleo – unemployment
el empleo – employment
las cifras – numbers / figures / statistics
financiero/a – financial
las finanzas – finances
la bolsa (mercantil / de valores) – (the) stock market
invertir (e → ie) (e → i) – to invest
el presupuesto – budget
los impuestos – taxes
la responsabilidad – responsibility
beneficiar – to benefit
el beneficio – benefit
donar – to donate
juntar fondos – to gather funds
recaudar fondos – to raise funds
aplicar (para) / solicitar – to apply (for)
rico/a – rich
pobre – poor
la pobreza – poverty
garantizar – to guarantee

los países (y nacionalidades) hispanohablantes
Europa (europeo/a)
    España (español/a)
Norteamérica / América del Norte (norteamericano/a)
    Estados Unidos (estadounidense)
    México (mexicano/a)
Centroamérica / América Central (centroamericano/a)
    Costa Rica (costarricense)
    El Salvador (salvadoreño/a)
    Guatemala (guatemalteco/a)
    Honduras (hondureño/a)
    Nicaragua (nicaragüense)
    Panamá (panameño/a)
El Caribe (caribeño/a)
    Cuba (cubano/a)
    La República Dominicana (dominicano/a)
    Puerto Rico (puertorriqueño/a) (estadounidense)
Sudamérica / América del Sur (sudamericano/a)
    Argentina (argentino/a)
    Bolivia (boliviano/a)
    Chile (chileno/a)
    Colombia (colombiano/a)
    Ecuador (ecuatoriano/a)
    Paraguay (paraguayo/a)
    Perú (peruano/a)
    Uruguay (uruguayo/a)
    Venezuela (venezolano/a)
África (africano/a)
    Guinea Ecuatorial (guineano/a)

otras palabras y expresiones útiles
insistir (en) – to insist (on)
mostrar (o → ue) – to show
demostrar (o → ue) – to demonstrate
completar – to complete
cumplir (con) – to comply / to follow through (on)
exigir – to demand
reprimir – to repress / to suppress
prohibir (i → í) – to prohibit
eficaz / efectivo/a – effective
esperar – to hope (for)
esperar (a) – to wait (for)
la expectativa – expectation
unir(se) (a) – to unite (to get together / to join)
reunir(se) (u → ú) (con) – to reunite (to meet up with)
romper / quebrar (e → ie) – to break
aportar / contribuir (y) – to contribute
ofrecer (c → zc) – to offer
admirar – to admire
acabar de + *infinitivo* – to have just _____ ed
acabar (con) – to end / to stop / to put an end (to)
sino + *sust.* – but rather (used for contrast w/ "*no*")
    no esto, sino eso – not this, but (rather) that
sino que + *verbo* – but rather
sino también – but also (in addition w/ "*no*")
    no sólo esto, sino también eso – not only this …
estar a favor (de) – to be in favor (of)
estar en contra (de) – to be against
los pros y (los) contras – pros and cons
sugerir (e → ie) (e → i) – to suggest (recommend)
valorar – to value
valer (yo valgo) – to be worth
el / la mismísimo/a – the very same
entre sí – among themselves (ellos / ellas)
    – among yourselves (Uds.)
dominar – to dominate / to be fluent in a language
hispanohablante – Spanish-speaking
hispanoparlante – Spanish-speaking
de habla hispana – Spanish-speaking
de habla española – Spanish-speaking
anglohablante – English-speaking
angloparlante – English-speaking
de habla inglesa – English-speaking

expresiones que requieren el subjuntivo
ojalá (que) – hopefully / god (Allah) willing
para que – so that
con el fin de que – so that (with the goal being that)
a menos que – unless
a no ser que – unless
con tal de que – provided that
acaso que – in case
sin que – without

Unidad 30 – los refranes, los modismos y las expresiones idiomáticas

estar entre la espada y la pared – to be stuck between a rock and a hard place

todo va viento en popa – it's smooth sailing

por las buenas o por las malas – come hell or high water / by hook or by crook / one way or another

a fuerzas – no matter what

para lo bueno y para lo malo – for better or for worse

de la sartén al fuego – out of the frying pan and into the fire

tener la sartén por el mango – to have things under control

ir de mal en peor – to go from bad to worse

de pies a cabeza – from head to toe

blanco y negro – black and white

una cuestión de vida o muerte – a matter of life or death

pedir peras al olmo – to ask the impossible

a otro perro con ese hueso – don't piss down my back and tell me it's raining

de tal palo, tal astilla – the apple doesn't fall far from the tree

del dicho al hecho hay un buen trecho – it's easier said than done

dime con quién andas y te diré quién eres – you are who you hang around

allá donde fueres, haz lo que vieres – when in Rome, do as the Romans do

en boca cerrada no entran moscas – loose lips sink ships

tarde o temprano – sooner or later

no hay mal que por bien no venga – every cloud has a silver lining

llover a cántaros – to rain cats and dogs

zapatero, a tus zapatos – mind your own business / let the cobbler stick to his last

cada quien a lo suyo – every man for himself / everyone for themselves

a cada quien lo suyo – to each his own / to each their own

dar la vuelta a la tortilla – to turn the tables

la prueba de fuego – trial by fire

al pie de la letra – by the book / verbatim

echar leña al fuego – to add fuel to the fire

poner el dedo en la llaga – to add insult to injury / to pour salt in the wound

tomarle el pelo a alguien – to pull someone's leg

comerse el coco – to go nuts (crazy) (thinking about something) / to rack one's brain

perder los estribos – to fly off the handle

media naranja – better half (used to describe one's spouse, soul mate, etc.)

dejar a alguien con la palabra en la boca – to cut someone off (when s/he is speaking)

en la punta de la lengua – on the tip of one's tongue

un callejón sin salida – a dead end

una espada de doble filo – a double edged sword

mandar a alguien a freír espárragos – to tell someone to go fly a kite

mi casa es su casa – make yourself at home

como Pedro por su casa – like he owned the place

hogar, dulce hogar – home sweet home

el / la niño/a de mis ojos – the apple of my eye

matar dos pájaros de un solo tiro – to kill two birds with one stone

yo que tú / yo, en tu lugar – if I were you / if I were in your shoes

sano y salvo / sana y salva – safe and sound

a lo largo de (tiempo, muchos años, etc.) – over the course of (time, many years, etc.)

antes muerta que sencilla – I wouldn't be caught dead wearing that.

colorín colorado este cuento se ha acabado – that's all she wrote

un don nadie / una doña nadie – a nobody

otro cero a la izquierda – a good-for-nothing / a nonentity (like another zero left of the decimal 00.1) un/a fulano/a (de tal) – a so-and-so (a non-specific or theoretical person – "a John" or "a Jane")

un/a sabelotodo – a know-it-all

meter la pata (meter las cuatro) – to put your foot in it (to really put your foot in it)

el mundo es un pañuelo – (it's a) small world

en un dos por tres – in no time / in a flash / in an instant

cada dos por tres – every now and again

dejar plantado/a a alguien – to stand someone up (like for a date)

seguir en pie – to still stand (plans) / to hold up (not fall through – plans) / to still be on (plans)

la edad del pavo – tween years / early teenage years

a paso de tortuga – at a snail's pace

perder el hilo – to lose one's train of thought

¿Cuánto te va a costar el chiste/la broma? – How much is the thing gonna set you back?

(hay que) ver para creer – seeing is believing (you'll have to see it to believe it)

a estas alturas – at this point

por puros golpes de suerte (un golpe de suerte) – by sheer/pure luck (a stroke of luck)

estar hasta la coronilla – to be fed up / to have had it up to here (hand gesture at head level)

manos a la obra – get to work / let's get to work

por si las moscas – just in case

por encima de mi cadáver – over my dead body

pagar los platos rotos – to pay the piper / to clean up one's mess (figuratively)

rendirle cuentas a alguien – to be held accountable to someone

como buscar una aguja en un pajar – like finding a needle in a haystack

hay gato encerrado – there's something they're not telling me / there's something fishy going on

sudar la gota gorda – to sweat bullets

hacer la vista gorda / hacerse de la vista gorda – to turn a blind eye / to look the other way

pasar por alto – to overlook

meterse en camisa de once varas – to stick one's nose where it doesn't belong

caminar por la cuerda floja – to walk a fine line / to walk a tightrope

menos mal que … (*indicative verb*) – it's just as well that …

trágame tierra – kill me now / just shoot me (when embarrassed or overwhelmed)

que te parta un rayo – damn you / a pox on you (a curse on whomever the object is)

maldita sea – dammit (damn it)

al fin de cuentas / al fin y al cabo – when it's (is/was) all said and done / when it's (is/was) all over

de cabo a rabo – cover to cover (book) / from beginning to end / from start to finish

a espaldas de alguien (a mis espaldas) – behind someone's back (behind my back)

ponerle los cuernos a alguien – to cheat on someone (in a romantic partnership)

cerrar el pico – to shut one's trap

como si fuera poco – as if that weren't enough

costar un huevo – to cost a fortune / to cost an arm and a leg

darle mala (buena) espina a alguien – to give someone a bad (good) feeling

de una vez por todas – once and for all

empezar la casa por el tejado – to put the cart before the horse

en ascuas – on tenterhooks / on pins and needles / on the edge of one's seat

morderse la lengua – to bite one's tongue

poner las cartas sobre la mesa – to put all the cards on the table

salir el tiro por la culata – to backfire

ser pan comido – to be a piece of cake (easy)

tomar a pecho – to take to heart

ir al grano – to get to the point

cortar por lo sano – to cut one's losses

cada ocho días (cada 15 días) – every week (every two weeks)

de mañana en ocho (de este lunes en ocho) – a week from tomorrow (a week from this Monday)

de todo un poco – a little bit of everything

un día de estos – one of these days

a bote pronto – off the cuff

ponerse las pilas – to buckle down

a solas (con) – alone (with – always with someone or something)

el pájaro de mal agüero – bird of ill omen / bearer of bad news

más vale pájaro en mano que cien volando – a bird in the hand is worth two in the bush

más vale tarde que nunca – better late than never

micha y micha – split it 50/50

frente a frente – face-to-face / head-to-head

ser como uña y mugre (uña y carne) – to be like two peas in a pod / to be (as) thick as thieves

agarrado/a con la mano en la masa – caught with his/her hand in the cookie jar

reír a carcajadas – to laugh out loud

echar/tirar la casa por la ventana – to spare no expense

estar a mano / estar en paz – to be even / to be square (no one owes the other anything)

pegar ojo – to get some shut-eye

pasar la noche en vela – to have a sleepless night

a mi mejor saber y entender / a mi leal saber y entender – to the best of my knowledge

los abajo firmantes (afirmamos, expresamos, etc.) – (We) the undersigned (affirm, express, etc.)

que sueñes con los angelitos – sweet dreams

ponerse al tanto – to wise up / to get with it

decir algo sin pelos en la lengua / no tener pelos en la lengua – to not mince words

tener cara de pocos amigos – to scowl

mejor solo que mal acompañado – (it is) better to be alone than in bad company

no saber (entender, hablar) ni papa – to not know (understand, speak) the first thing (about a subject)

no tiene (ni) pies ni cabeza – I can't make heads or tails of it / it doesn't make any sense at all

esparcir la voz – to spread the word

¿En qué quedamos? – Where do we stand? (on a deal, decision, etc.) / Where does that leave us?

¿Qué más da? – What difference does it make? / What does it matter?

na na na y no sé qué / no sé qué y no sé cuánto – I don't know, whatever, blah blah blah

Había una vez … / Érase una vez … – Once upon a time …

se me pegaron las sábanas – "the sheets stuck to me" (a humorous excuse for getting out of bed late)

San Lunes – "Saint Monday" (a fictitious holiday cited as the reason for not going to work on a Monday)

más sabe el diablo por viejo que por diablo – with age comes wisdom

dar en el clavo – to hit the nail on the head

¿Me entiendes, Méndez, o te explico, Federico? – Do I need to explain it to you?

ser para chuparse los dedos – to be finger-licking good

hacerse agua la boca – to make one's mouth water

estar (sentirse) como gallina en corral ajeno – to be (to feel) like a fish out of water

estar como pez en el agua – to be in one's element

pase lo que pase – whatever happens / no matter what happens

perro ladrador, poco mordedor – his bark is worse than his bite

el tiempo es oro – time is money

hacer hincapié – to dig in one's heels / to put one's foot down

andar con pies de plomo – to proceed with caution

echarle una mano a alguien (con algo) – to give someone a hand (with something)

ser de carne y hueso – to be flesh and blood

algo por el estilo – something along those lines

con uñas y dientes – tooth and nail

a cámara lenta – in slow motion

los trabalenguas
Tres tristes tigres se tragan trigo en un trigal.
Ere con ere – guitarra, ere con ere – barril. ¡Qué rápido ruedan las ruedas del ferrocarril!
Pablito clavó un clavito. ¡Qué clavito clavó Pablito!
Pedro Pérez Pereira, pobre pintor portugués, pinta preciosos paisajes para poder partir para París.
Poquito a poquito Paquito empaqueta poquitas copitas en pocos paquetes.
Como poco coco como, poco coco compro.
Pepe Peña pela papa, pica piña, pita un pito, pica piña, pela papa, Pepe Peña.
Me trajo Tajo tres trajes, tres trajes me trajo Tajo.
Parangaricutirimícuaro

un poco de humor grosero
No es lo mismo: "la papaya tapatía" que "tía, tápate la papaya".
No es lo mismo: "los huevos de araña" que "aráñame los huevos".
No es lo mismo: "huele a traste" que "atrás te huele".
No es lo mismo: "el SIDA tiene cura" que "el cura tiene SIDA".
No es lo mismo: "la verdura" que "verla dura".
No es lo mismo: "tengo un hambre atroz" que "tengo un hombre atrás".
No es lo mismo: "tubérculo" que "ver tu culo".
No es lo mismo: "dos tazas de té" que "dos tetazas".
No es lo mismo: "un metro de encaje negro" que "un negro te encaje un metro".
No es lo mismo: "Cenote Dos Ojos" que "¡Ojo, dos senotes!"

About the Author

David Faulkner holds bachelor's and master's degrees in Spanish, with an emphasis in teaching, and has taught Spanish in every grade from fourth to the university level. He is passionate about the fundamentals of language, as well as interpersonal communication and personal expression, particularly where their practical application has a positive impact on people's lives.

Faulkner opened up about his childhood in his memoir, *Superheroes* (2015), and has since shifted his focus back to his true calling: teaching Spanish and inspiring others to practice it in their daily lives.

Faulkner enjoys spending time with his family, public speaking, traveling the world, and staying active. He is an idealist and a relentless dreamer, reveling in the happiness of pursuit. *De cabo a rabo* (*Gramática*, *Vocabulario*, and *Actividades*) comprises his second, third, and fourth books.

To schedule David Faulkner for a curriculum presentation to see how his Spanish guides could benefit your language program, or to hire him for private lessons or as a guest teacher at your school, please contact him through DavidFaulknerBooks.com.

Flashforward
Publishing

Made in United States
North Haven, CT
04 January 2022

14189932R00043